C000016272

ON
MY
WAY
HOME

One woman's journey in search of
the unknown God

Deborah Armin

Authentic

Copyright © 2015 Deborah Armin

21 20 19 18 17 16 15   7 6 5 4 3 2 1

First published in 2015 by Authentic Media Limited
52 Presley Way, Crownhill, Milton Keynes, MK8 0ES.
authenticmedia.co.uk

The right of Deborah Armin to be identified as the author
of this work has been asserted by her in accordance with the Copyright,
Designs and Patents Act 1988.

All rights reserved. No part of this publication may be reproduced, stored in
a retrieval system, or transmitted in any form or by any means, electronic,
mechanical, photocopying, recording or otherwise, without the prior
permission of the publisher or a licence permitting restricted copying.
In the UK, such licences are issued by the Copyright Licensing Agency,
Saffron House, 6–10 Kirby Street, London, EC1N 8TS.

British Library Cataloguing in Publication Data
A catalogue record for this book is available from the British Library
ISBN: 978-1-78078-130-3   978-1-78078-267-6 (e-book)

Scripture quotations are taken from The Holy Bible, New International Version®
(Anglicised edition). Copyright © 1979, 1984, 2011 by Biblica (formerly
International Bible Society). Used by permission of Hodder & Stoughton
Publishers, an Hachette UK company. All rights reserved. 'NIV' is a
registered trademark of Biblica (formerly International Bible Society).
UK trademark number 1448790.

Some names have been changed to protect the identity of the individuals
concerned. However this is the true story of my life and all other details have
been presented as accurately as memory allows at the time of writing.

Cover design by David Smart smartsart.co.uk
Printed in Great Britain by CPI Books (UK) Ltd., Croydon, CR0 4YY

I'd like to dedicate this book to the Lord Jesus Christ, thank you for never letting go of me.

Acknowledgements

I'd like to thank everyone who's been a part of my journey, each person has had a part to play, without you it would not have been the rich history it is, without you I would have been a lot poorer.

Contents

Prologue

It was the year 2000, but it felt to me as if the Twin Towers had already come down. Not literal towers, you understand, but the structures I had built in my heart.

I had given my heart to 'Mr Charming' but that had ended. And with it the tower of love had imploded.

To make matters worse, things had deteriorated between my best friend and me. She had disapproved of my relationship with Mr Charming and I had disapproved of her relationship with a married man because it had stirred painful memories about what my dad had done. Things had never been the same between us after that. Something had broken and it felt as if the tower of friendship had come falling down too.

As I sat in my living room in Florida, I realized that I was now very much alone. I had only recently moved to the 'Sunshine State' and the new friends I had made were busy with their own challenges, and I didn't want to bother them. I knew from my own experience that to burden friends too soon with your problems was the kiss of death. When you're up, new friends love you. When you're down, they run like panicked crowds.

In any case, I was sick of hearing myself talking about all the same old issues.

And I didn't want to listen again to the same old clichés and platitudes thrown like stones at me:

'There's plenty more fish in the sea.'

'Maybe a hobby or another little job would help.'

That last comment had really bruised me. As if my job as a professional massage therapist didn't count!

So I really was alone. There was no escaping it.

My old friends were too dispersed and distant geographically.

My family were thousands of miles away in England.

I had never felt so desolate.

Tears were falling down my cheeks.

My heart felt as if it was being suffocated under heavy rocks and thoughts were tumbling like debris into my head.

'You're a loser!'

'You're alone.'

'You're trash.'

I sat on my sofa, hunched over my lap, trying to take cover, desperately seeking shelter from the emotional devastation all around me.

I didn't know what to do or where to turn.

All I needed was a hug from someone I trusted. Just a hug and the words, 'It's going to be OK, Deborah.' But there was nothing.

Just silence.

The sun had gone in.

My apartment felt empty.

I was falling down.

Falling . . .

Falling . . .

Falling . . .

And I couldn't stop.

There was only one thing for it – a huge dose of sleeping pills, like I'd considered before. Only this time, I would make sure I did it properly. This time my sleep would be permanent.

But I didn't move from the chair.

No sooner had I made the decision than something – or someone – stopped me. I never even stood to go and fetch the tablets. It was as if I was glued to my sofa and all I could think about was the indescribable agony my suicide would cause to my family and friends.

In an attempt to take my mind off all this, I reached for the remote and switched on the TV. I landed on the God channel where a lady called Joyce Meyer was teaching from the Bible and inviting people to say what she called 'the sinner's prayer'.

I had nowhere else to turn.

There was nothing to lose by praying.

I stumbled vaguely through the words but my mind was full of turmoil.

I opened up my Bible – the very one Mr Charming had bought for me the previous Christmas – and tried to read, but my eyes were so full of tears it was difficult.

I put the Bible down and cried out.

'If you're really real then I need you to come to me right now! I need you to show up for me because if you don't I'm going to end it all. I can't take any more. I feel destroyed.'

As I said that, I hit bottom.

I felt desperate.

I was at ground zero.

Part I
Leaving Home

1

Age of Innocence

Given that for many years I have been on a spiritual journey, it's fitting that I was apparently conceived near Stonehenge, a place that's always been a magnet for mystics, travellers and spiritual seekers.

Nine months later I was born in Portsmouth. The year was 1965, so now you know my age. It was 5.30 p.m. and I arrived just in time for tea, or so my mum jokingly says. I quickly became fond of tea as a toddler – so fond, in fact, that I earned the nickname 'Puddles' on account of the small pools I left everywhere around the house.

Dad was at that time stationed at a naval base near Stonehenge and spent a long time away from home. My mum was left for extended stretches to cope with three children under the age of 10. It was tough for her.

As I grew up, I remember Mum saying that I had been 'a surprise' and that she'd tried to stop her pregnancy by drinking gin and vigorously cycling up a hill – though not at the same time, presumably. Later she would say to me, 'Well, at least I didn't have an abortion.'

These comments didn't exactly make me feel as though my arrival had been celebrated, or that my life had been welcomed.

I forgave my mum a long time ago because I came to understand the immense pressures she had been facing, not least the fact that she was effectively bringing up her children as a single parent.

But the words still hurt.

And they left a legacy of rejection and insecurity.

Mum did her very best with precious few resources. She had little help except occasional support from my Nan. We moved often, but she always somehow managed to keep the new house clean and tidy and there was always food on the table. She created a warm home wherever we went.

I'll always be grateful to her for that.

As for Dad, he wasn't around a lot, but whenever he was he gave mixed signals. On the one hand he was adventurous and the source of fun. On the other he was strict and critical, and his behaviour was often scary.

'Do you want to be as stupid as your brother?' he would say, as he used to correct my homework.

To this day he corrects me on my spelling or my choice of words, although now I get my own back by correcting his as well.

'Touché, Da!' I'll say with a smirk when I catch him out.

From early on I had this hunch that there is far more to life than can be seen. This intuition grew particularly strong in times of emotional turmoil and family stress. At those times I felt that something or someone was watching over me, but I had no idea what or who. Since my parents weren't religious, I had no framework for understanding this sixth sense, no language for it, either.

But I wanted to know.

When I was 4 years old, we moved to a semi-detached house in Somerton in Somerset. It had three bedrooms and Mum kept it meticulously clean. Dad refurbished the kitchen in pine wood. I remember watching *Dr Who* with him. There was a long garden behind the house with a stream at the bottom. I played for long hours there.

I am sure I had been having dreams for a long time but now, in Somerton, I began to remember some of them. Most of them were not very pleasant; they tended to be about people trying to kidnap and kill me.

One dream in particular stood out. It was about someone trying to murder me using bleach. My mum used bleach a lot when cleaning the house.

When I woke up the smell of bleach was still in my nostrils and my throat felt sore.

Some might be tempted to say that it was simply my mum's cleaning products that brought this on. But it felt as if there was more to it than that. It seemed significant to me.

As did other dreams, especially ones in which I was being kidnapped. Where had they come from? And what did they all mean?

Neither my mum nor my dad appeared to be spiritual people, so there was no religious talk in our home. We didn't discuss phenomena such as dreams and yet I knew instinctively that they were important.

Only much later did mum start saying that she had psychic abilities. She also started referring to astrological star signs, saying 'You're a typical . . .' or 'that's so typical of a . . .'

She would study the stars in popular magazines and newspapers and read out my star signs to me – something which would later fuel my interest in astrology.

At 4 years of age, however, all this was in the future.

I was ignorant about such things.

And when it came to the knowledge of good and evil, I was still innocent.

But that was about to change.

2

Close Calls

It was in my fifth year that I first became aware that I was living in a dangerous world.

We had just moved to South Africa. Dad had retired from his job in the navy and was now employed by South African Airways. We had moved roughly once a year in my first five years and were now living on another continent. Looking back over my life, I've worked out that so far I have moved sixty-five times in under fifty years.

When we arrived in South Africa we initially moved into an apartment in a block of flats which surrounded a communal garden and a swimming pool. It was sunny and very warm and the garden was full of flowers.

Our apartment had two doors – a front door which was the main entrance and exit and a back door which led to the stairwell and the fire escape.

One day when I was out playing on the stairwell an older boy tried to get me on my own.

'Hi, I've made a present for you,' he said. 'Do you want to come with me?'

I followed him into a neighbouring flat where he gave me a flower ring.

Then he tried to kiss me.

I fled.

I didn't see him again but the experience frightened me. I had felt the presence of something evil for the first time in my life.

I didn't go out the back door into the stairwell for another week. When I did eventually venture out, a dark-haired white man started following me.

He was my dad's age, about mid-thirties. He spoke to me in Afrikaans but I didn't understand. I knew he wasn't safe, however, so I ran back upstairs into the shelter of our flat.

Not long afterwards, Mum found out that a paedophile was in the block and had been arrested. She told me not to talk to strangers any more.

Many years later I would look back on this incident and realize that something or someone must have been watching over me, because I felt sure that the man who'd talked to me had been the same person who was arrested. I had had a close brush with evil and the thought of that sent a shiver down my spine. In fact, from that time on I was constantly aware that evil might be lurking not far away and that danger was just around the corner.

And it was.

Remember I said that there was a communal pool?

One day I was swimming with a friend of the family who offered to give me a piggyback across the pool. All of a sudden she was seized with cramp and she dropped me. I sank straight to the bottom. I hadn't learnt to swim yet and I began to gulp water. I tried to breathe, but of course all I did was take in more water. It was most surreal – as if I was out of my body watching myself sink.

The next thing I knew, someone was grabbing hold of me from behind and bringing me back up to the surface.

'That was a close call,' I heard someone say.

As I lay beside the pool coughing up water, I sensed something watching over me. In all the chaos, there was this strong, protective presence.

In fact, from a very young age I became constantly aware of two forces – a threatening, sinister power intent on harming me, and a watchful, overshadowing presence equally intent on protecting me.

It was during this brief spell of living in the block of flats that I started attending Sunday school for the first time. I don't remember much, I have to confess, but I do have a vague memory of hearing about this man called Jesus. Since we moved quickly after that, I only attended a couple of times so I heard no more about him.

The place we lived in next was a bungalow. It had a garden which I loved playing in. I became convinced that there were fairies living among the flowers. Once again I was captivated and enchanted by things unseen. Even though this was a subject my parents never talked about, I just knew that there was an invisible, spiritual world all around me – just a gossamer thread away.

Inside the bungalow it seemed dark and foreboding. I didn't like it at all and never felt secure there. I always felt as if there was a shadow following me.

The garden outside was my green zone. It was a bright, warm and safe place. There was so much to fascinate me, including a chameleon on the grapevine. I had never seen one before. I spent hours looking at it.

I wasn't fascinated by these things for long, though. Very soon we were on the move again, to another bungalow which my parents had now bought.

If I had felt unsafe in the previous place, however, this new one was to be no better.

3

Reign of Terror

From a child's point of view, your father is your protector, your defender, your guard and your guide. He is the one who makes you feel secure, honoured and special. He is your knight and your hero. Even if the hordes of hell were to try to storm the doors of your house, you would feel safe, provided your father was standing in their way.

Once we moved to our new bungalow, I sadly began to realize that my father was not like this. It is hard to speak about these things because so much good has happened in our relationship since then and I really want to honour him. But at this time, when I was little and vulnerable, my father's behaviour was sometimes confusing.

To put it delicately, it was at this stage in my life that I started receiving mixed messages from him, especially in the realms of affection. These happened sporadically but they left their mark on me.

Dad used to take showers and baths with me and it was at these times that there was inappropriate behaviour.

All I wanted was my dad's love and approval. All I got was a dark and distorted expression of those things. I don't want to go into any more detail except to say this: these overtures of 'love' left me feeling very ashamed and defenceless.

Later on in my life, the legacy was, I'm afraid, destructive. I came to believe the lie that this was a normal way for a woman to receive love. When boys and men began to exploit me sexually, I mistook this for what true love is.

It would take a long time before I found healing from these old wounds.

The new bungalow was therefore not a safe place. Dad was absent a lot because of his work. When he was home he was not always affectionate in an appropriate way. He was not affirming of me either.

This hurt.

Looking back, I wish I had received some spiritual or moral guidance from my parents in those formative years. When I later got married in the 1980s, I began to realize how messed up I was and how I had allowed myself to repeat toxic relationships with men. That realization would lead me to seek counsel from New Age self-help books.

During my early years, however, my parents did not provide me with the spiritual and moral compass which might have saved me a lot of heartache. My dad even stated that he was an atheist. So the sum total of my religious input was the Sunday school classes I'd been to in South Africa.

One thing I do remember very vividly, however, was a comment from my mother.

'You're a little witch,' she said one day.

We were in the family car at the time and I was massaging Mum's forehead because she had a headache. I was singing a little chant that I'd made up.

'Wrinkles, wrinkles, go away, don't come back another day.'

I didn't know what the word 'witch' meant. But my mother's comment – which was meant to be playful – made an impression on me.

It was a momentary and rare incursion into the spiritual world by one of my parents.

That felt important.

I remember something else too. It all started when I saw something in my older sister Janet's room.

'Look,' I said to her.

'Look at what?' my sister replied.

'There are shadowy shapes in the corner of your bedroom.'

I was not joking or teasing. I could see them. But my sister was terrified, especially since this happened more than once. Sometimes I would stare at them for ages and make myself go bug-eyed. My sister and my friends couldn't see them and that made me feel different from everyone else. No one else mentioned seeing or feeling such things, so I learnt to keep quiet about them.

At the same time as I was seeing things from the spiritual world, as it were, family tensions were beginning to intensify in the new bungalow. That is not to say there were not moments of fun – such as horse riding and days out to zoos and animal farms. It's just that conflict seemed to increase, especially between my brother, Patrick, and my father.

One day, I found my father and my brother having a loud and violent argument in the hallway. This grew more and more hostile until both of them lost control and started to hit each other. Fists were flying everywhere.

I was already scared of my father.

Now I became terrified of him.

We all knew that he wasn't the most patient of people and that he also had a short fuse. But this seemed to be altogether different. This wasn't just anger. It was rage.

One of the worst moments for me was when he erupted one day at the dinner table. Our dog, Snoopy, was begging while we ate as a family.

Snoopy was an American beagle with typical black, white and tan markings. I absolutely adored her.

'Stop begging!' my father shouted one mealtime.

But Snoopy didn't take any notice. She continued jumping up at our legs and looking at our food.

The next moment my father grabbed Snoopy by the scruff of her neck, dragged her to the kitchen door, opened it roughly and then dropkicked the dog into the yard.

Snoopy yelped.

And I began to cry.

My father came back to the table.

'I told that bitch not to beg,' he shouted.

Then he sat down and looked at me.

'Stop crying,' he shouted, 'or I'll really give you something to cry about.'

Not long after this, the hostility between my father and brother eventually came to a head.

Patrick was ten years older than me so he was about 15 at the time.

The fighting between them escalated until one day my father said, 'OK, you can leave South Africa and return to England.'

'Where will I live?'

'You'll stay with your nan in Somerton,' my father replied.

No one explained to me why my brother had to leave, but leave he did. And from that moment on I came to believe that if I got into trouble I'd be shipped off to another country, never to return.

I was terrified.

And I was distraught. I was only 5 or 6 years old when my brother left South Africa.

I didn't understand what was going on.

And I don't even remember him saying goodbye.

4

Out of Africa

It was the 1970s and our stay in South Africa coincided with apartheid, a word that I'm told means 'the state of being apart'. In 1948 the National Party had created an official policy of segregation between the races – which were divided into four groups, 'white', 'black', 'coloured' and 'Indian'. The majority of the population was black but their rights were greatly curtailed by the minority ruling party made up of white Afrikaners. This reached a critical point in 1970 when non-white representation in the South African government was formally abolished. This created inevitable tensions, especially between the black and white inhabitants of South Africa. As the Black Consciousness Movement led by Steve Biko began to endorse black pride, relations between blacks and whites reached boiling point.

I didn't understand any of this at the time, but it did hit home for me personally when Constance, our maid, arrived one day with a terrible gash on her forehead, covered by a big bandage. When we asked what had happened, she told us that she'd been attacked on a train on her way to work.

'Why?' we asked.

'Because they found out that I work for a white family,' she replied.

I cried when I heard this. I loved Constance and I couldn't understand anyone wanting to hurt such a lovely person.

This incident was a tipping point for my parents. They had already become very anxious about the escalating violence and the increasing unrest in the country. What had happened to Constance was the last straw.

'Right, we're heading back to England.'

'But I want to stay here.'

'It's not safe.'

'Do we have to go?' I pleaded.

'Not forever, just until this all blows over. The family will be safer there. Dad will have to look for another job but it'll be OK. Don't worry.'

So back we flew to England to live at my Nan's flat.

My Nan was my mum's mum and was called Stella. She was short and thin with a slightly hunched back. She had a bad leg so her left knee often used to knock into her right leg.

She was very protective of me whenever we went out to the pub where she cleaned.

I remember her hands. Her palms were extremely soft but the backs were covered in protruding veins, it sounds strange but I loved to play with her veins!

Nan and I had a special connection. She adored me and I adored her and I enjoyed living with her. I was her favourite, according to Mum, and she took me everywhere with her, taking every opportunity to spoil me.

As a result I quickly got to know the area, and it wasn't long before I started exploring the local village on my own.

There was a large church behind the flat where my Nan lived. I often went into the ornate building and watched as the sun's rays poured through the stained-glass windows. The coloured images would throb with light and life while dust motes seemed to hang in the air of the sanctuary. Very often that sense of someone watching over me would return whenever I stared at the huge cross.

I couldn't stay too long though. Being totally alone I would often get scared and run from the old stone building. I would then wander through the graveyard examining the graves, reading the gravestones, preoccupied with death, fascinated by mortality.

We're only here such a short time, I'd think to myself.

I'd then saunter home with my thoughts. When my mum used to ask where I'd been, I'd say,

'I've been in the graveyard looking at the headstones.'

'That's my little witch,' she would reply.

This seemed to make my spiritual antennae even more sensitive.

One night I was sleeping in my Nan's room when I was woken with a start. There was a strange sound coming from outside the window. At first I couldn't figure out what it was, but then I remembered a similar noise. It sounded like a blacksmith hammering a horse's shoe on an anvil.

I climbed out of bed and snuck up to the side of Nan's bed to see if she had woken up too. But she hadn't. She was fast asleep.

I then tiptoed to the window and drew back the curtains. I gazed out onto the old street below with its cobblestoned pavements. I could see the archway of the old Red Lion Hotel where the horse-drawn carriages used to stop centuries before. This had been a place where passengers on the coaches could stretch their legs, drink ale and eat some hot crusty pie before continuing on their journey.

As I gazed into the darkness, I couldn't see anything that could have been responsible for the hammering sound so I closed the curtains again and crept back into bed.

When I started to drift off I had a strong image of an old man in a leather apron. He said something to me but I can't recall what it was. It startled me. In fact, I was so scared I found it hard to breathe. In spite of this, I soon fell into a deep sleep.

The next morning I told Nan what I had heard and seen, but she didn't comment and nothing more was said about it after that. I never did find out what the sound was, but I know that it wasn't made by human hands.

Still, I wasn't worried. I always felt safe when I was with Nan. I loved her dearly and I knew that she loved me too.

I wish I had been able to get to know her better, but constantly moving from place to place made things difficult. Most of the time she didn't live near enough for me to visit her on a regular basis.

This left me with a void in my heart.

I longed for an extended family, and seeing Nan partially fulfilled that longing.

Later on, as I grew up, I would seek to fill this hole by being drawn to large families – Italian, Hispanic, African, Asian and others.

It didn't matter to me what race or colour they were.

I've never understood racism and I've certainly never believed in apartheid.

I gravitated towards large families because I love the way they look after each other and spend time together.

For me, they have always been a great antidote to 'the state of being apart'.

5

Arabian Nights

It seemed no time at all before my father found a new job and
we were moving again. This time it was to Kuwait.

Kuwait was completely different from anything I had been
used to. Instead of living in a country struggling with poverty, I now found myself in one of the wealthiest countries in
the world – one made rich from its huge oilfields.

Southern Arabia couldn't have been more different from
South Africa. Most of its small land mass was covered in
Arabian desert. Dramatic sandstorms were from time to
time whipped up by the *shamal*, a north-easterly wind which
became particularly violent in June and July.

Then there was the sea. At the tip of the Persian Gulf, you
could see dhows everywhere – big wooden ships made of teak
imported from India.

At lunchtime – when families gathered together for their
main meal – you could smell the *shawarmas*, falafel and *machboos* everywhere. Machboos were especially popular – spiced
rice dishes with chicken, fish (usually greasy grouper) or
meat. After lunch you could detect a hint of mint in the
local tea and the strong aroma of Arabian coffee.

You could hear plucked lutes and drums, as well as the call to prayer from the mosques.

The women walked in black cloaks that seemed to cover most of their bodies. The men were dressed in white *dishdasha* – woollen or cotton garments that went down to the ankles. They wore headscarves folded into triangles, held in place by a circlet made of black cord. They would shake hands with each other and kiss one another on the cheeks.

All this was a new world for an English girl.

After a temporary stay in a hotel, we moved into an apartment opposite the beach. I instantly fell in love with the dazzling sunshine glinting on the surface of the sea.

I loved the warm climate.

In fact, I loved everything about the place.

Every week we would drive out to our favourite remote beach and see camels walking in the middle of the road and Arabian horses loping through the desert, their tails riding high in the air, their flanks lathering in the sun.

We took trips to souks or bazaars that were like something out of Aladdin's cave and sailed in a dhow past the blue water towers being built in Kuwait City.

Even walking around the fish stalls was an adventure, leading us to try many new meals. In fact, ever since then, I've loved fresh hummus, samosas and pitta bread.

There was just so much to take in, it was breathtaking.

I'll never forget first hearing people speaking in Arabic, or the sound of a man calling out from the beautiful mosque with its tall tower nearby.

An airline pilot in our block of flats explained to me that the man was calling people to prayer. I remember being both intrigued and disturbed. Part of me longed to go inside the tower to find out what mysteries lay there. Another part of me felt there was something eerie about it all.

In spite of all these different and new sights, sounds and smells, I just knew deep down that all human beings are basically the same in terms of their needs – fresh air, water, food, shelter and especially love.

I knew that it didn't matter what we look like on the outside, what colour we are or what we wear, all of us have the same basic need to love and be loved.

So it was sad that as a family we were seemingly incapable of fulfilling that need.

It was tragic that we were capable of ugliness in a landscape of such beauty.

Thus it was that my father continued his inappropriate displays of affection to me, including at the beach one day where snorkelling with him turned into something altogether shocking.

And then there were the parties. Dad had his own bar in the living room so alcohol was served, which was illegal in Kuwait. During these evenings my father would confide in me that he found certain women attractive.

'How would you like her as a mother? Don't you think she's sexy?'

I remember being so confused when I heard him talk like this. Didn't he love Mummy any more? Was she going to leave, like my brother, Patrick, had?

What was I to do?

Perhaps if I went along with what he was doing, then I wouldn't be sent away. But then the guilt and shame afterwards were almost unbearable.

This feeling of insecurity became even more intense when my sister Janet left us too.

Once again no one told me what was going on or why she was leaving.

All I knew was that Janet wasn't going to be living with us. She was to be flown back to the UK and placed in a boarding school.

And so, like Patrick, she left. I had no way of keeping in contact. There were no mobile phones, no email, no texts, no Skype – nothing except airmail letters. That was a lot for an 8-year-old to deal with. I was far away and alone with my parents.

To add to the unhappiness, my parents were now arguing a lot, and their rows were beginning to frighten me.

It was about this time, however, that I found comfort in an unexpected source. A relative of mine sent me a children's picture Bible as a present. I was so excited when I received this big and colourful book. Whenever I felt afraid by my parents' arguments, I would go into my room and hold the book. Instinctively I knew there was something special about it and I would flick through its pages and find solace and serenity while emotional and verbal storms were raging around me.

Often my parents would go out to a neighbour's flat for some drinks. Instead of hiring a babysitter they would simply lock me in alone. Sometimes I would sense a sinister presence and look under my bed to check that there wasn't someone in my room. Again, when I felt this way, I would intuitively know that my book had the answer and I would look at it again and calm down.

Except whenever I reached the place where the man was so terribly badly hurt and then violently killed.

That would upset me deeply.

I would always end up crying.

I didn't know why he had to die.

So in the midst of a completely non-religious family, in a Middle Eastern country, love – True Love – was reaching out to me.

Not the kind of love that my father was showing.

No, this was a different kind of love.

This was an otherworldly love – a safe, soothing, pure and tender love.

Love was stretching out a hand from another dimension, from beyond the stars and beyond the sea.

Indeed, one night I remember sitting in bed in the front bedroom, the one with a balcony overlooking the ocean. It was my favourite room in the flat, although not the room where I normally slept.

I was reading the big book and I reached the part where the man was being cruelly abused and I cried out, 'What have we done?'

As I said those words, I immediately sensed this strong, kind, and reassuring presence. It didn't frighten me at all.

And I had the faintest sense that there was someone else in the room – a man dressed in a radiant, white robe.

6

Passage to India

When I was about 10 years old, I began to have more and more mysterious spiritual experiences.

One morning I woke up in the front bedroom of our apartment in Kuwait. This might not seem altogether unusual, but the truth was, I had gone to sleep in the back bedroom!

At breakfast I asked my mum about this.

'Do you know how I ended up in the front bedroom?'

'Yes. I saw you floating from the back bedroom to the front bedroom in the middle of the night.'

'Floating – are you serious?'

'Yes, I was in the bathroom at the time, looking out into the hallway. You were floating several inches off the floor.'

As if that wasn't strange enough, another time I was lying in bed about to fall asleep when I heard the sound of a man's voice. It came out of thin air; there was no one else around. My parents and my brother (who was visiting) had gone out to a party. As usual they had locked me in and left me alone.

The voice was not a pleasant one.

'Don't move,' it snarled. 'Or I'll come and get you.'

I was rigid with fear.

I looked around my room.

There was no one there.

I didn't dare move an inch.

I held my breath as best I could, trying not to make any noise.

I don't know how long I stayed like this but it must have been several hours, until my brother, Patrick, returned. After that I finally felt able to move. I had been paralysed with terror and was numb all down my back.

Another moment I vividly remember was when I was standing in front of my Barbie dolls' house. I was merrily playing with my Barbies when suddenly I spoke these words: 'I just want to wear white, no manmade fibres, just linen or silk or cotton. I want to be pure.'

At the same time as these experiences seemed to be on the increase, I was making some new friends. One of these was a girl called Fatima. Both her parents were doctors and they owned a private hospital in Kuwait City. Their apartment was high up at the top of the hospital.

One time I was staying with Fatima when her mum arranged for me to get my ears pierced. I was so excited. Their Indian maid used ice on my ears before pushing a needle through them. She then put beautiful gold and amethyst earrings in. I felt so grown up and so happy with my friend's gift.

Fatima's mum also arranged for me to have a traditional outfit made, and when it was ready we went to a wonderful party held at a relative's home. The house was beautiful. The interior was breathtakingly glamorous. I'll never forget the gilded furniture and the magnificent chandeliers.

I loved Fatima and I enjoyed spending time at her house. The only time this was not the case was the day I took the small private lift down from their apartment and it got stuck. I was terrified, all alone in the lift. It had only descended a couple of floors so I knew I was still very high up. Thankfully it wasn't too long before I heard men shouting, 'We're going to try to pull you out!'

What a relief it was when they managed to pull the lift up to the next floor and I escaped through the doors that they had forced open.

Perhaps the most unforgettable experience I had at this age was a trip to India. My parents were planning to leave Kuwait and return to England. Before that, my father decided we should take a holiday in India.

When we arrived I was overwhelmed by it all – the colours, the saris, the coloured bracelets, the beautiful people, the ornately carved wood, the endless variety of flowers. It was all such a feast for my young eyes.

And then there were the aromas – curry spices, different kinds of incense, and of course the flowers which seemed to adorn everything from altars to cows – all of which covered the smell of the dirty and overcrowded streets.

We stayed at the Taj Mahal hotel in Bombay opposite the Gate of India. While we were there, I met another English girl whose Indian father was a doctor. He had brought his English wife and daughter to visit his family.

'Would you like to come with us and experience real Indian food and customs?' they asked.

'Yes please!'

It was so much fun. The ladies at the house dressed me in a sari and put lots of bangles on my arms. Then they put a bindi mark on my forehead and said prayers over me. I had no idea what they were praying or its spiritual implications. To me it was all a bit of harmless fun. After the prayers, we ate chapatis and played with handmade dolls which the ladies gave me when I left. I had a great time.

A few days later I was out at the hotel pool when a wedding took place. I was mesmerized by the flowers and the clothes. The smell of incense wafted through the garden. It was stunning.

That same day, my mum was in the beauty salon and one of the women, an Indian lady, took my hands and began to speak to me. The only part I can recall now is that she said I had 'special hands'. Later on in my life I was to use these 'special hands' in my job as a massage therapist.

Not everything I saw and heard in India was beautiful. Outside our luxurious hotel I couldn't help observing people with leprosy on homemade skateboards, trying to get about without the use of some of their limbs.

The level of poverty was unreal; people were left to die at the side of the road. I saw one lady hitch up her sari and defecate in the middle of the street.

It struck me as so strange that big cows with garlands wrapped around their horns wandered freely amongst the traffic. The people – many of whom were starving – couldn't eat these beasts because they were revered as sacred.

I also couldn't understand why there were so many poor people. Where were the people to take care of them? The huddle of tin shacks they called home seemed so miniscule and dirty. They reminded me of the shanty towns I had seen in South Africa. It felt so wrong and I wondered why they weren't able to have proper homes.

When I asked why this was happening, I learnt from the doctor about *karma* (the poor are poor because of what they've done in previous lives) and, of course, the caste system. But I was really too young to understand it all.

To make it even more confusing, I also saw many temples and statues where people were lighting incense and bowing in veneration, while outside these shrines and altars there was chaos, poverty and such sickness.

One day, while waiting for a boat by the Gate of India, I was surrounded by a large crowd of children, begging. I myself was just a child yet I felt moved and gave away all of my pocket money.

The experience touched me deeply.

I felt so sorry for them.

I wished I could do more.

As we travelled back to Kuwait to prepare for our return to England, I couldn't get the memory of these starving children out of my head.

Why was there so much suffering?

But then I was about to discover that my family was not immune to pain either.

7

The Break-up

As soon as we returned to Kuwait, the fun of India began to feel a million miles away as the relationship between my parents deteriorated.

My father, in particular, became more and more angry and abusive.

I used to dread doing homework with him. He was so impatient with me and quick to criticize my efforts. I was a slow learner and needed to do exercises several times before fully understanding them. My dad just didn't like that, and used to make cutting remarks about me being stupid.

But it wasn't just me that suffered at Dad's hands. My mum was the one who really got it in the end.

It all took a turn for the worse one awful New Year's Eve. My parents had gone to the flat upstairs for a party. I was allowed to go to part of the celebrations before being brought downstairs and locked alone in the flat.

I must have fallen asleep after a while because I suddenly woke up to the sound of my parents arguing in the bedroom next to mine. I had no idea what time it was. All I could hear was the sound of them shouting.

I lay on my bed afraid until there was a period of silence.

Then suddenly my dad started yelling obscenities at my mum and she began to scream at him. I could hear thumping noises. I didn't know what to do. It sounded as if my parents were killing each other.

I climbed quietly out of bed and went into the adjoining bathroom that I shared with my parents. I looked through the open door and saw my mum at the end of the bed with my dad behind her. To my horror I saw him grab hold of her hair and punch and kick her from behind.

Terrified, I screamed out to them to stop and then ran from their bedroom into the living room. My mum ran after me, yelling to my dad to stop. She grabbed hold of me and tried to use me as a shield.

As she did I caught sight of her face.

It was black and blue, covered in bruises.

Just as I thought my dad was going to attack us both, a lady from upstairs came to our door and took Mum and me to her flat while some men talked to my dad.

Things quietened down until morning, but the next day my mum's eyes were swollen almost shut. I'd never seen anything like it. She had to hide behind huge sunglasses.

The next thing I remember, Mum and I were at the airport and on board a plane bound for England.

I would never go back to Kuwait to live. And my father didn't come with us.

I was to visit my father only once. He flew me to Kuwait, and because I was travelling alone the stewardesses put me in first class to keep an eye on me. I even got to go in the cockpit because Dad knew the pilot.

When I arrived in Kuwait I met Dad's girlfriend. She was a woman I knew who lived upstairs in the block of flats. Her husband was also a pilot.

The following Christmas, Dad came to visit us in England. I was happy to see him even though I was also confused.

He decided to surprise me by buying me a big Christmas present.

Dad made me go into the bathroom and wait before I was led into the living room where there was a brand new piano. It was incredibly exciting. I had always loved music and wanted to take lessons. I also longed to impress Dad so that he would love me and come home to stay.

But it was not to be.

Dad had no intention of staying, even though it looked to me for a while as if he might.

What we didn't know was that Dad had secretly brought Mum's clothes back from Kuwait and shoved them into the back of her wardrobe. She didn't find them until he'd returned to Kuwait. When she did, she was devastated.

So was I.

I had suspected that he wasn't coming back when he had told me that he wanted me to be his 'brick'. He told me I had to be strong because he wanted to be with his new girlfriend. He had even asked me what I thought of her.

I was only 12 or, at the most, 13 at the time.

How was I to answer that? I was desperately confused and upset. I had so many unanswered questions.

What is Dad saying?
Why is he leaving Mum and me?
Doesn't he love me any more?

It was a phone call that finally ended any lingering hope in my heart.

I'll never forget it.

The phone was ringing in the kitchen. I was sitting at the table trying to do my homework. Cliff Richard's song 'Summer Holiday' was playing on the radio. Everything seemed normal.

But then Mum answered the phone.

It was Dad.

Mum's voice cracked.

She began to wail into the receiver, shouting 'Why? Why? Why?'

My blood ran cold.

Mum slumped to the floor.

The receiver just hung there.

I ran over to her.

I picked up the receiver. My dad spoke to me but I don't remember what he said. His message was obvious. He wasn't coming home and he wanted a divorce.

Later my sister came home and Mum tried to explain to her what had happened. I ended up in tears and ran out of the kitchen. My sister ran after me as I raced down the hallway, trying to escape the pain. I flung myself on her bed and she tried to console me.

From that moment on, my mum was permanently distressed. She went on and on about my father. My sister wasn't around much and my brother was never there so I absorbed everything.

I became exhausted by it.

I rarely heard from my father in the years that followed.

There were a few letters with some pocket money but one day they stopped abruptly, without explanation.

My father had bought me a piano for Christmas. I had been willing to take lessons because it pleased him. I practised on it often because he always used to say, 'See you in Carnegie Hall, babe.'

After my parents divorced, I never played it again.

8

School of Hard Knocks

My piano and I separated not long after my parents divorced. We had moved to a town called Yeovil in Somerset. I hated the move because it meant not only leaving Nan, it also meant that I had to say goodbye to my closest friend who lived on a farm next door and with whom I used to go horse riding. I loathed moving from a beautiful country village to an ugly town and I detested being the new girl in a new school yet again.

I didn't realize it at the time, but the harsh reality was we had to move. Dad was now out of the picture, so Mum had to sell our bungalow and find us a new and affordable place to live, as well as apply for jobs and benefits so that we could survive. As much as I hated it, looking back I'm proud of my mum for the way she rescued the situation. She made many sacrifices to create a lovely home and fine meals.

But she also understandably became very emotional. After a while, it began to get on my nerves, especially when I wanted to share my own pain with her.

'Well, now you know how I feel,' she would retort.

This made me feel as if I had to experience her suffering on top of my own.

It also made me feel as if it was always about her.

Never once did she ask, 'How's all this affecting you?'

My piano is a good example.

We had brought it with us to Yeovil and it now stood in our living room. It made me too sad to play it, so it was not being used. I hadn't found a new piano teacher in town either because I wasn't sure I wanted lessons.

I wasn't ready to get rid of it and it wasn't taking up an inordinate amount of space; it rested against a wall behind the door to the living room. But my mum started to have a go at me.

'That piano of yours is taking up too much room. You never use it. I'm sick of it being there. It's getting in the way. It's time to sell it.'

This went on for a while and in the end I caved in. I had been so torn because it was the last thing my dad had given me. It was an emotional trace belonging to him alone. But it had to go, so I sold it.

I can still remember crying when it went.

I was about 14 at the time.

It was about then that I was trying to settle into my new school in Yeovil. There was this one boy who used to tease me relentlessly. I would dread bumping into him, but then I became best friends with the headmaster's daughter. She was small in stature but acted as a shield between me and the bullies.

I found it tough to focus on my studies. Not only was there the stress of the teasing, I was also trying to cope with the trauma of my parents' split and us moving. All the dramatic changes in my life had taken their toll. I was not concentrating as well as I could, and I was not receiving any guidance about setting goals and choosing subjects.

I was just left to cope on my own.

Things weren't all bad, though. It was at this time that I started to grow in my understanding of the spiritual or religious dimension to life.

At my new school we had an excellent Religious Education class, and I remember a number of times feeling really touched during various discussions. I often felt as if my teacher was speaking directly and exclusively to me whenever she talked about Jesus Christ. I recognized him from my illustrated children's Bible – which Dad had ditched when Mum and I abruptly left Kuwait – and I remember feeling as though I knew him.

It was partly this spiritual sensitivity that made me something of an oddball at my school. I had started midway through the year so that hadn't helped. I had also travelled widely and when I shared my stories with others they just thought I was weird. In spite of my new friends, I did feel like a loner and found it hard to settle. In the end I decided to keep quiet about many of my experiences.

Perhaps it was this feeling of being an outsider that was partly responsible for me starting to go out drinking with some of my mates after school. I didn't feel as if I belonged anywhere so this was probably a symptom of that. Drinking stopped me thinking too deeply and also helped me to relax, to feel more confident and to fit in.

At the time I didn't feel good about myself.

'You're too tall and it's impossible finding suitable clothes for you at the shops,' my mum would say. 'I can't buy you fashionable clothes because I can't find ones that fit you, why do you have to be so big?'

As a result of all this, I felt unusually awkward and unattractive. This hardly helped when I was experiencing the normal teenage angst about whether I was pretty or anyone fancied me!

However, the drinking boosted my self-confidence and I began to be known for being cool and a good laugh, much to the dismay of my teachers.

Just as life seemed to be changing for the better, however, things took a turn for the worse.

Our financial situation as a family was really tight so I had to clean tables every Saturday at the café where my mum worked. This in itself was not bad. It was the fact that all the kids from my school would come into town to do a bit of shopping and they would stop at the café for a laugh while I had to clean their tables.

That was humiliating. I just wanted to dig a hole in the floor and vanish.

In the end, I struggled through my exams, not knowing what I wanted to do after graduating from school. I was still too preoccupied with the hurts from my past to get motivated or excited about my future. Finally I managed to pass several 'O' levels and CSEs.

I was so relieved when it was over.

But then we received some terrible news.

Nan had died.

I knew she had a heart problem because my mum and I had been to her flat after she had had what was believed to be a heart attack. We had followed the ambulance to the hospital. Later we visited her on the ward. She seemed to be OK.

But then in the middle of the night, Mum received a phone call from the hospital.

Nan had passed away.

Mum and I clung to each other and wept in each other's arms.

I couldn't believe she'd gone.

I had expected her to recover.

I thought that I'd get to see her again.

I felt winded.

When I went to the crematorium for her funeral, everything seemed a blur. It all felt so surreal. I couldn't talk to anyone. I was just too choked.

When I went to bed I woke up in the middle of the night. I could feel my nan's presence in the room. I could detect her familiar aromas – the smell of her talcum powder and the peanuts she used to love munching. She had gone but it felt as if she was still there.

No one explained to me what happened to people after they died.

There was no talk of heaven.

I received absolutely no counselling or comfort.

As always, life just had to go on.

9

Beauty Treatment

If I'm honest, immediately after I left school I didn't have a happy time. In the subsequent years I went through the nightmare of a broken engagement and the trauma of two abortions.

After I graduated I joined a local college and enrolled on a course devoted to business studies. This was really my mum's doing. She had told me she was worried that I didn't have sufficient skills to find a good job. So off we went to the local College of Further Education to have a chat with an administrator there. She suggested I did the business studies course so that's what I did.

But I hated it.

It wasn't me.

I was bored.

And I felt lost in many of the classes.

Consequently, I looked for excitement in all the wrong places, going out in the evenings and at the weekends with my then best friend, 'Miss Fashionista', from Zimbabwe. She and I would drink and dance until the early hours of the morning and then on occasion I'd sleep with men whom we'd randomly met.

This was our regular routine.

If I was looking for drama, it wasn't long before I was confronted by it head-on.

One day, after going to the gym at the college, Miss Fashionista and I were crossing the road from one side of the campus to the other. There was a main road on a hill going through the two sides of the college. As we got to the curb, we both looked out for traffic, but our view was obscured by all the cars parked either side of the road.

I took a few steps into the road.

Suddenly my friend was screaming at me, 'Watch out, Deborah!'

But it was too late.

A Volvo which had been travelling down the hill smashed into me. I had a split second to see it coming, but it was all a blur. I saw part of the car then felt searing pain as it smacked into my right thigh, catapulting me up onto the windscreen.

My head smashed into the glass and I blacked out.

I came round to find myself on the road in agony.

I felt pain everywhere.

Miss Fashionista was in hysterics.

The driver of the car was screaming that it was my fault.

My sailing instructor from the college held my head, trying to keep me still. He thought I'd broken my neck.

As I lay there on the ground, I remembered the sinister and malevolent voice I'd heard in Kuwait. It was saying, 'I will kill you.'

I was rushed off to hospital and X-rayed, given an aspirin, a full leg bandage, and sent home. I had a huge haematoma on my right thigh and every part of my body hurt.

It wasn't until a couple of weeks later, when I complained I was having trouble walking, that the hospital realized they hadn't X-rayed all of my leg so they did a more thorough job and discovered a broken fibula. So now a full leg plaster cast was fitted.

It took weeks for the leg to heal, and by that time I was so far behind with my studies at the college that I decided to quit. I didn't have the strength or incentive to go back and catch up.

I was alone the day the police came to the house to take a statement about my accident. I ended up telling them I didn't want to press charges. Later I found out that the man driving had been a local teacher and he had just come from a Christmas party where he had got drunk.

Life moved on after I left my course. I found a job in a jeweller's shop. It was a bit boring but I've always loved a bit of bling so there were some compensations.

Then Mum found a new boyfriend and I realized we needed to go our separate ways. I left home and moved in with my boyfriend. I also decided it was time for some further education and a decent job.

So off I went to the job centre.

And when I got there I did something that I'd never done before in my life.

I prayed to the unknown God – to the one I knew had been watching over me all my life. I prayed to the God whose name I didn't know, whose existence I couldn't prove.

After I'd finished praying I began to browse through the adverts in the job centre. In those days they had cards pinned up on boards. These cards had details of the jobs or training available.

I stood in front of one board and in my head asked the unknown God, 'OK, what am I meant to be doing?'

Straight away a card advertising beauty therapy training seemed to stand out. I had always loved anything to do with the body – beauty, biology, you name it. So I took the card down and went to the desk to ask about it.

There a woman told me I could apply for a student grant to go to the college and enrol on the course. She helped me with the forms. My curiosity was aroused. It was as if I was in the flow of something bigger than me. I was so excited; I felt as though I would finally have some direction in my life and that I'd be working towards achieving a qualification in something I had always liked. The qualification was to become a CIDESCO Aesthetician. This covered all aspects of beauty therapy, facials, eyelash tinting, manicures, pedicures, waxing, and electrolysis, diet and massage therapy. At the end of it I'd be a qualified beauty therapist.

There was only one fly in the beauty ointment, however – my fiancé.

He and I were living together in Yeovil at the time. The college I wanted to go to was in Plymouth, a drive of over three hours away. This would mean that we'd be separated a lot from one another during term time.

How was he going to react to the news?

When I broached the subject he was none too pleased.

'Why do you want to leave me?' he pleaded. 'Aren't I good enough?'

'Of course you are,' I replied. 'It's just that I need to go on this course. I love the subject. This is what I want to do in the future.'

'But why do you want to change everything? Why can't you be satisfied with what you have now?'

'I don't want to change everything. I just want to get qualified for something I love doing, and to do that I have to go to Plymouth.'

'Well, I know what's going to happen.'

'What?'

'You'll probably meet some preppy guy there and end up going out with him.'

Nothing I could say would calm him down. I had had absolutely no intention of looking at other men. My sole motivation had been a deep longing to improve myself. I was ambitious and wanted to get somewhere in life. But my fiancé's insecurities were raging.

Eventually he calmed down and reluctantly agreed.

'OK, you can go,' he said, 'but I bet you meet some toff and fall in love with him.'

'I won't,' I insisted.

I tried everything to reassure him that he was my man.

'Why don't you come down to Plymouth whenever you can? We'll be fine. You'll see.'

I left my fiancé in Yeovil and moved to Plymouth to join the course. I stayed in a boarding house where the landlady only took in girls attending the college. It helped enormously to have a motherly figure there. I was terribly homesick and missed my fiancé. It was a tough transition from living with him in Yeovil and then moving miles and miles away, only being able to make phone calls. My heart ached and I felt vulnerable. Here I was branching out, trying to improve my life, but I was alone again.

To alleviate the loneliness I threw myself into my studies. I enjoyed the subject and felt I was a natural at it. Everyone started saying my massage and facials were the best. It felt really good to be complimented and, apart from my struggles with chemistry, I was quite confident in my capabilities.

But then I was hit by a bombshell.

My fiancé had cheated on me pretty well as soon as I'd left for Plymouth.

I was devastated.

But after many tears, I decided it was time to move on with my studies and get qualified.

I managed to get through my exams and completed the course.

I was so pleased with myself that I had managed despite the drama that had gone on. I set about applying for jobs in beauty salons and spas, or 'health farms' as they were called in those days. It seemed like an eternity waiting for a job. In the meantime I had to go to the job centre to look for work, something I detested doing. They never seemed to understand who I was and what job would fit my personality or my qualifications. It was very frustrating.

I tried various jobs, including work as a barmaid – anything to avoid signing on the dole. But none of these brought satisfaction and in every case I ended up compensating for the tedium by clubbing and getting drunk, even while money was really tight.

I continued to look for a job in beauty therapy. And while I was looking, the nearest thing I could find to working in the beauty industry was selling perfume.

It was just a means to an end.

It wasn't what I really wanted to do.

But it paid the bills.

So if you once had some tall girl spray perfume at you, you never know – it might have been me!

10

Visiting a Psychic

You'd think that after all the moves I'd made I'd have been used to being made homeless. But I wasn't. Part of the problem was that the news came out of the blue. I had moved out of the boarding house into a shared flat with two of the girls from my beauty therapy course, but not long after moving in, my flatmates had for some reason failed to inform me that our lease had run out and the landlord had asked us all to leave. The other two had decided to rent a new place with their respective boyfriends and had therefore made alternative arrangements. They had not thought to tell me.

However, it seemed that yet again someone or something was watching over me. I had made a wonderful new friend, an Indian girl who had fled from an arranged marriage. She was going to be sharing a large Victorian house with another friend and they allowed me to stay with them.

I loved 'Miss Sunshine'. She was a sweet girl who had a smile that could light up a room. She loved having fun so we three girls went out clubbing when we weren't working. The house where we lived was beautiful so coming home was always a joy.

Everything went smoothly until one day the other girl fell madly in love and suddenly decided it was time to move out of our house and move in with her boyfriend. This left Miss Sunshine and I high and dry, barely able to pay the bills. We temporarily took in another lodger but she failed to keep up the payments so we asked her to leave.

Then one day Miss Sunshine dropped a bombshell.

'Deborah, I've got something to tell you.'

'What is it?'

'I'm pregnant.'

'What!'

'I've been seeing this guy.'

'You kept that very quiet!'

'Yes, I'm sorry. It's just that I really wanted to get to know him properly before I introduced him to anyone.'

As it turned out, the reason Miss Sunshine had hushed it all up was because the man was married and she was too ashamed to tell me.

She and I continued to live together in the house and I continued to look for jobs in the beauty industry, but to no avail.

I was beginning to lose hope when one day Sunshine asked me if I'd like to come with her to see a psychic. That was not something I had ever done before and I was more than a bit sceptical. But since I had not lost any of my curiosity about the unseen spiritual world, I agreed to go. I had no intention of getting a reading; I was just there for Sunshine, her moral support.

That evening we walked miles to the house of a lady who did psychic readings. When we went in I noticed a cross on some shelves.

After inviting us into her house she said, 'Please wait out-side,' to me, while she led Sunshine into her front room.

While Sunshine was inside, I began to ask questions.

What's life all about?

Who am I?

What am I here for?

What's going to happen to me?

Where's my life heading?

As I sat pondering, the door opened and Sunshine came out. It felt as if she'd only been in the room a few minutes. As the psychic lady walked out she looked me in the eye.

'I have something to tell you,' she said. 'Would you like to come in for a reading?'

I was a bit taken aback, yet something inside of me leapt at the idea. But I didn't have any spare cash. How was I going to pay for it?

'Don't worry,' she said, 'I'll do it for free.'

She had read my thoughts!

I followed her inside.

The reading when it came was brief.

'I see you travelling across a large body of water. You will meet and marry a man with dark hair and you will be known for the work you do with your hands.'

That was it!

I thanked her and walked out in a bit of a daze.

That was the first time anyone had seen and said anything so precise about my future. Still, at the time I thought it was all a load of nonsense. After all, there was nothing even remotely like that on my horizon. 'Crossing a large ocean – that's ridiculous,' I thought.

I tried to brush it off but the truth was my spiritual antennae were now twitching.

Maybe there was a future for me across the sea.

Maybe there was something I didn't know and hadn't seen.

It was to be a sudden and familiar disruption that proved the catalyst for unexpected changes in my life.

Miss Sunshine and I were finding it very hard without a third tenant to pay the bills. One day the landlord told us we had to move out straight away, with no notice.

We sat at the kitchen table eating toast and drinking tea, trying to figure out what to do.

'Where are we going to live now?' she said.

'I don't know,' I replied. 'It all seems so unfair.'

I was 20 years old and fairly resilient. But this seemed a trial too far. The landlord conceded and had given us just two days to leave. It was going to be tough finding a new home. And yet, I still sensed someone or something was watching over me and that everything would be OK.

Eventually Sunshine found a place to live but it only had room for one person. This left me scurrying to the housing benefit office. A lady there pointed me in the direction of a shared house with a room that was available to rent. I moved in but it wasn't a pleasant place. It was a large Victorian house like the one we had been living in, but this one was dark and unfriendly. I hated it.

I ended up taking my sister's offer of moving to Wales to live with her, so yet again I was on the move, tossed into uncertain waters.

While all this was going on I couldn't help harking back to what the psychic had said to me, wondering how and when I would be crossing an ocean, marrying a dark-haired stranger, and developing a reputation for working with my hands.

My present circumstances seemed far away from that possibility. I just couldn't see how it could ever happen.

I decided to turn to the unknown God once again.

'I'm not sure who you are or if you're real,' I said, 'but if you are, I'd really appreciate a sign right now – just something to give me a bit of direction.'

By now I'd found a job working in retail, and during my lunch break one day I decided to read a copy of the daily newspaper that a colleague had left lying around.

I turned to the job section.

'Nanny needed in New York.'

I sat up with a start.

'Nanny needed in New York,' I read again.

It was only a tiny advert but it seemed enormous to me. It felt as if it had zoomed up into my face, causing everything else in my vision to become blurred.

'Nanny needed in New York.'

'I'll never be someone's nanny,' I tutted to myself. 'No way!'

But I couldn't get the advert out of my head.

That day I went home and left the newspaper at work.

When I returned the next day, the newspaper was still there, exactly where I'd left it. Normally someone would have removed it and thrown it away. But for some reason it was still lying on the table and still open at that same page!

I just knew I was supposed to apply for this job.

I had never done any work as a nanny, only a spot of babysitting.

But I had an inner compulsion to pursue it.

I picked up the paper and ripped out the advert.

I then phoned my sister and told her what I was doing.

'The only thing is,' I said, 'they want someone with experience.'

'That's OK,' she replied. 'I can ask my best friend to say that you were a nanny for her family.'

I submitted the application and to my amazement I received a letter inviting me to go to London for an interview in one of the fine hotels just off Hyde Park. The whole experience made me feel special.

The person who interviewed me was the mother of the lady whose children needed a nanny in New York.

'We are Hasidic Jews,' she said, 'and very Orthodox.'

'That's fine with me,' I replied.

'You will have to learn how to obey kosher laws,' she added.

I didn't have a clue what that meant or what the future held but my horizons were already broadened from all the travelling I'd done so I agreed.

When I walked out of the interview I just knew the job was mine.

I was very naïve about what moving to a foreign country and working there really entailed. I should certainly have asked many more questions. I didn't think about – or realize – the fact that I would be an illegal worker. I was young – now 21 – and also adventurous.

As I said farewell to my mum and my stepdad at the airport a short while later, it all felt very surreal but also extremely exciting.

I couldn't help remembering the words of the psychic.

'I see you travelling across a large body of water.'

If that was now unexpectedly coming true, maybe the rest would too.

Maybe my beauty therapy vision would take off and I'd have a reputation for working with my hands.

Maybe there was a dark-haired handsome man waiting for me across the ocean.

Part II
Far from Home

11

Escape from Brooklyn

'She won't be back,' my sister said to my mother.

The plane had taken off to the USA and in no time at all I was landing in New York. I had been told to go through to the arrivals hall and look out for a name written on a card. However, when I got there I couldn't see it anywhere.

What have I done? I thought.

Just as I was beginning to feel the onset of panic, I heard a woman's voice.

'Deborah?'

I turned and there was a lady with black bobbed hair, dressed from head to toe in black. Her face was pale and she had an appearance different from anything I had ever been used to. For a moment I wondered if she had been seriously ill and her hair was a wig.

I followed her out of the terminal and to her car. Her driver was also dressed entirely in black and had long twirls of black hair at the sides of his head, tucked behind his ears. He had a tall black hat which reminded me of the ones worn in the cowboy movies I used to watch.

At that time I knew nothing of the customs and traditions of Orthodox Jews. Later I was to discover that it was part of their beliefs not to cut their hair in that area and to cover their bodies for the sake of modesty. I was also to discover that the lady, who was my boss, *was* in fact wearing a wig.

I climbed into the long black stretch limo enjoying a fleeting feeling of importance. We drove through the streets of New York until we arrived at a large house in Brooklyn. The windows of the car were smoked so it had been hard to see the sights. However, I do recall that it was an extremely built-up area, and when we arrived at my boss's neighbourhood I also remember thinking that there were a lot of other people who looked like my fellow passengers.

I was fascinated.

Who are all these people?

Why are they dressed in such an old-fashioned way?

When we entered the house I was taken straight to my ground-floor bedroom. Given the size and the opulence of the residence, I was expecting a spacious room with perhaps its own bathroom. Not so! I discovered to my surprise that I was in fact sharing a room with the 1-year-old twins I was going to be helping to look after.

Once I had unpacked I went upstairs and my induction began. I was told the rules and given strict instructions about what was expected of me.

I just wanted to cry and get on a plane back to England.

It was all too strange and it was all too much.

I was 21 and had gone from being an independent, free-spirited and adventurous individual to being trapped in a small room, dressed in long-sleeve shirts and skirts, forbidden to talk to men, and not permitted to bring anyone to the house. On the Sabbath – from Friday sunset to Saturday sunset – I was not allowed to watch TV, listen to the radio, or use light switches.

It was a massive shock to my system.

Even simple acts like cooking food for the children had unfamiliar rules and regulations. I had to use two different sides of the kitchen – one where I could use dairy products and the other where I could prepare and cook meat. The two were never to be mixed.

Pretty soon these regulations felt like suffocating restrictions.

I was not allowed to use the phone without permission.

If I went out with the children it was for a specified and strictly limited time.

My passport was removed for 'safekeeping'.

And I was suddenly informed that I would have to work my first four weeks without being paid, in order to pay my boss back for the cost of the flight over to the States.

I was stunned.

That night I cried myself to sleep.

Everything seemed designed to make me feel like an imprisoned foreigner. Even language seemed to accentuate the problem, with my boss and her husband refusing to speak English when I was in their presence. They spoke Hebrew instead.

How am I going to get out of this nightmare?

I wrote letters to my family and friends to try to seek help and advice. My boss said she'd post them for me through her husband's office. One day, however, I was folding the laundry and putting it all away in her wardrobe in neat stacks when I cut myself on something.

Ouch!

I lifted the stack of sweaters and found my letters. I'd got a paper cut!

They had all been sliced open with a knife and had been hidden at the back of her clothes.

Not one of them had been posted.

Now I was scared.

Why has this woman confiscated my passport?
Why has she taken my jewellery as well?
Why did she open my letters?
Why didn't she post them?

Not long afterwards I even discovered that she had been listening in on my telephone conversations. I was always told to use the phone downstairs. She would dial the number for me upstairs and then tell me to pick up. Several times I'd heard a strange noise on the phone and on other occasions she would make reference to what I had said to my family. I had always been surprised by this because I thought my conversations had been private.

But they weren't.

And I was now feeling extremely exposed and vulnerable.

But I wasn't going to give in.

I was going to fight.

I had always been a fighter and I just knew that there had to be a way out of this dreadful situation.

Plus I still had that sense of someone or something watching over me and that everything would work out OK.

Over the next few days I learnt smart tactics and I learnt them quickly.

I managed to exchange some English money for US dollars at a local store. I made several calls from a payphone while out with the children on our daily walks.

Away from my boss's prying ears, I contacted a friend nicknamed Tigger from Wales. She was a lovely girl and had become very interested in my new venture in the USA. So she had decided to sign up to a nanny agency and had initially been given a job in California. She was slightly disappointed because she'd wanted to come to New York. Luckily for me, at the last minute the agency had changed their minds and decided to send her to New York instead. She was now in Manhattan so she spoke to her new boss about my plight.

In the meantime, I did my job as a nanny to the best of my ability and tried to stay out of the house as much as I was allowed.

I felt trapped and I hated it. My hosts were unbearably cold and I felt so confined it was hard to breathe sometimes. They made me feel worse by telling me that they'd had an English nanny before and that she had been very happy, which made me feel that it was all my fault.

In an effort to offset the loneliness I tried to be friendly towards some of the ladies I met on the streets, but they were frosty towards me too. If I dared to smile at or say hello to a man they would literally cross the road to avoid me, or scowl at me.

I tried to get to know the other woman working in the house as a cleaner, but she was Polish and couldn't speak a word of English.

Sometimes, however, you don't need words to communicate effectively.

One day, while helping her to do the chores while the babies slept, I went to one of my boss's wardrobes in another bedroom which she used as her personal dressing room. I was looking for the cupboard to put away her clean bed linen. I opened a large wardrobe door and was greeted by heads and eyes staring back at me.

Maybe these are the heads of previous nannies!

I screamed, dropped the laundry and ran.

When the Polish maid heard me, she laughed and took me back into the room, and it was then I realized they were the heads of manikins. Through sign language, the grinning maid conveyed to me that these were the boss's wigs. Evidently a married Jewish woman in that tradition had to cover her natural hair with wigs and scarves; only her husband was permitted to see it.

And the restrictions didn't stop there.

The maid took me through to the boss's bedroom and showed me not only that she and her husband slept in two single beds, but that they also could only be intimate together through a hole in a special sheet.

I was shocked!

It wasn't long after this episode with the wigs that I found my way into a phone box to talk with Tigger who was now in Manhattan.

'Deborah, there's good news!' she said.

'What?'

'My boss's best friend lives in upstate New York and she needs a nanny.'

'Wow!'

'If you can get over here for an interview with my boss, you've got a good chance of getting it.'

'Ah, well that might be tricky.'

'Why?'

'I haven't been given a day off since I came to Brooklyn. I'm not sure if I'll be able to get out.'

'Can't you at least try to persuade your boss to let you out for the day?'

'Yes, I'll give it a go.'

Later that day I approached my boss and asked her if I could take the next day off. At first she was sceptical and said I wasn't allowed to leave Brooklyn, but in the end she relented and said I could have time off. I was relieved. I had no idea how to get to Manhattan but I had seen a train station on one of my walks.

It can't be that difficult.

The next day I used what little cash I had to find my way to my friend's apartment in Manhattan. I was so relieved to see a familiar face. Tigger's beaming smile was such a tonic and in no time at all we were catching up on our news.

The family she worked for seemed so normal in comparison to what I had been used to – friendly too. When Tigger's boss asked if I would like to work for her best friend, I thought to myself, *If she's anything like you, yes please!*

We agreed that I would go back to Brooklyn and I would tell my boss I was leaving. Then I'd get a taxi to the train station and take a ride to Katonah, upstate New York, where my new boss lived.

That was easier said than done, of course.

When I arrived back in Brooklyn, I confronted my boss.

'I'm sorry, but I'm not happy here so I'm handing in my notice and I'm leaving tomorrow,' I said. As my boss's jaw dropped, I continued. 'I want my passport and my jewellery back and I want one week's wages too.'

'You're not leaving!' she replied.

'Yes I am,' I retorted.

'You're staying right here.'

'Look,' I said, bringing out the big guns, 'if you don't give me my things and let me go then I will find the nearest police officer and tell him that I'm an illegal immigrant, that you've been holding me against my will and that you've stolen my personal identification documents as well as my belongings. I mean it. I will do it.' (By now I had learnt that I was an illegal immigrant.)

For a moment my boss looked shocked. She then calmed down and looked at me. 'I'll phone my husband and ask him to bring your passport home.'

'Why? Where is it?'

'It's in his safe at work.'

First thing the next morning a taxi arrived to pick me up. I hadn't slept a wink all night and the tension in the house had been awful. I had my bags packed and was ready to go. I also had a week's wages which I'd managed to persuade my boss to give me – a small miracle.

After a major detour to Atlantic City, with a taxi driver who had decided I was to be his date for a day out at the casinos (that's a story for another book), I arrived back at the train station.

I caught a train and sat looking out of the window. I had called Tigger the previous night to let her know that I would be travelling to Katonah and I gave an approximate time for my arrival, but due to the crazy episode in Atlantic City I was now extremely late and becoming anxious.

At the same time I was so relieved to be leaving Brooklyn. That had not been a home at all for me.

Now I was on my way to a new home.

I was free.

12

Out of the Frying Pan

I fell in love with Katonah even before I was able to see it. Arriving late at night, the contours of the village were obscured by the darkness, but I could make out that it was the complete opposite from what I'd just left and that it was a quaint suburban town with excellent amenities.

My new boss's husband picked me up. He was a tall man with a beard. He was not in the best of moods because I was much later than we had agreed. I felt a little scared of him, but I resolved to say sorry for being late and hoped that by morning it would all be forgotten.

When we arrived at his house I was shocked by how many trees surrounded it. Brooklyn had been a concrete jungle, but this was green and leafy. The home was a wood-covered ranch on a hill near a lake. Once inside I was overjoyed to find I had my own bedroom and en-suite bathroom.

I was in heaven.

My new boss was lovely too. She was a little short with me to begin with because of the late hour. But then she gave me a beaming smile and a welcoming hug.

What a contrast to the boss in Brooklyn.

The next morning I met the children and they were adorable – a 4-year-old girl and a new born boy.

In the clear light of a new day I could see that their home was beautiful, and extremely large. I had never lived in such a mansion before. My boss's husband – who was a big-wig in the advertising industry – had obviously done well. This had allowed my boss to become a stay-at-home mum. She needed me to provide the childcare so that she didn't become a 'stuck-at-home' mum.

In the early stages I enjoyed being with this couple and their children. They seemed so perfect. The husband was dark-haired and handsome and his wife pretty, petite and blonde. The home was idyllic and their lives seemed to be flawless. After Brooklyn, I was so relieved. But first impressions can be so deceptive.

Within a short space of time, cracks began to appear beneath the surface of this apparently innocent family portrait. The husband, in particular, became a nightmare. He began flirting with me and I found myself in a constant battle to resist his advances. When I wouldn't give in to him, he started taunting me. Then, when Christmas came and I was missing my home and family, he began to tease me about it.

During these weeks, my boss and her husband went out whenever they wanted to, but it was left to me to find my way to the town when I had the opportunity to do so. My boss didn't show me how to get there. Stuck in the middle of nowhere, at least as it seemed to me, I was totally dependent on her to show me some kindness. But that was slow in coming and I felt confined to barracks.

Eventually my boss decided I had better have driving lessons and a US driving licence so I could get out and about. I was so happy I cried. I knew it meant that I would be able to take the children out and that I'd also be able to have at least something of a social life.

Not everything was now rosy. The husband was bullying me from time to time and I was afraid of him. Then there were his arguments with his wife, which made me feel very uneasy. I just tried to get on with my job and ignore it. He was just an angry and argumentative man.

I felt increasingly alone. I just wanted some friends, but my boss never introduced me to any of her friends who had children. Eventually she set up some play dates for me. It was such a relief to have some company. I loved the children and never minded when they cried or had tantrums. But not having friends was hard. I was only 22 at the time and I hated being so cut off from civilization.

Thankfully I also managed to visit my friend Tigger. We hadn't been able to see much of each other because her family spent most of their time in Manhattan. However, they decided to buy a second home not far from Katonah. This was great news. Once I had learnt how to drive I was given the use of a small car and I was able to go to visit her. I felt like a new woman.

The only downside was my boss's husband who was continuing to flirt with me. One night he showed up at my bedroom door. He had entered without knocking. I was naked because I was about to have a shower. I nearly died. Luckily I was able to grab my towel which was lying next to me on my bed. I couldn't wait for him to go and it seemed like forever until he did. As soon as he had gone I locked the door. I was shaking.

My bedroom was above their double garage and was connected to the main house by a single passageway. I would have had nowhere to run. And yet I still had a sense of someone or something watching over me so I refused to let it get me down. By now I had started writing letters in my journal to the unknown God, to whom I gave the name 'X'. I had no idea who it was but I just sensed that I was being protected and that I would be OK.

It was, however, a struggle.

I lasted a few more months with the family but by Christmas it had all become too much.

I handed in a month's notice to the wife just after Christmas Day.

I apologized to her. 'I need to be in a job that's closer to people,' I said. 'I feel too isolated out here.'

'Well, I'm not happy,' the wife said. 'In fact, I'm mad as hell with you. My husband will be furious.'

And he was.

'You're a selfish, thoughtless, idiotic child,' he bellowed at the top of his lungs. 'If you think I'm gonna let you stay in my house and eat my food while being a traitor to us all, you've got another think coming!'

He continued to shout and threaten me, reducing me to a quivering, tearful wreck.

'I'm so sorry,' I kept repeating.

But it was to no avail.

He just kept on venting his anger at me, not allowing me to get a word in edgeways, while his wife cowered in the doorway of the living room to which he had summoned me.

Finally, he lost all control.

'I'm not gonna let you stay in my house another minute!' he exclaimed, threatening to throw me out the front door into the freezing winter night.

'Please, please, help me,' I shouted to his wife. 'Don't let him do this.'

'I'm sorry,' she said, 'I didn't expect him to react this way, but there's nothing I can do. I'll drive you to the train station.'

I ran up the stairs to my bedroom to gather my things.

My head was spinning.

Where am I going to go?

What am I going to do?

Who can I call for help?

After fifteen agonizing minutes, the wife came upstairs.

'Look,' she said, 'I've managed to persuade my husband to let you stay a few more days so that you can pack properly and find somewhere else to go.'

'Thank you.' I shivered. 'But what do you honestly expect me to do? All my friends around here are nannies like me who live in their boss's homes. They won't be able to have me.'

But my pleading made no difference. My situation was desperate. I had no family in the USA. I had no contact at that time with my dad. If I'd rung my mum, I know what she would have said: 'I'm very sorry about your situation, but there's really no way I can help you. You'll have to sort it out yourself.'

But sorting it out was not going to be straightforward. I had very little money because I had used any spare cash to get to and from Manhattan as often as I could on my days off. Now I was being thrown out by a bad-tempered man whose advances I had resolutely refused.

How am I going to get out of this one?

Two days came and went. On New Year's Eve, the wife confronted me.

'When my husband comes home from work today, he doesn't want to find you still here.'

'But what am I going to do?'

'I don't know. But you can't stay here.'

I felt numb.

I didn't know people could be this heartless.

I remember looking at the wife and thinking, *Don't you realize I'm someone's daughter, someone's sister? What have I done to you and your family to make you so cruel? Don't you realize it's freezing outside? Don't you care? I'm a human being, but you're treating me as if I'm worse than worthless.*

My last resort was my Welsh friend Tigger in Manhattan.

I phoned her to ask for help but she couldn't. Her boss was the best friend of my boss, who was in the process of throwing me out!

It was now time to leave.

'Please let me say goodbye to the children,' I said to the wife.

'No, that's not gonna happen,' she replied. 'I don't want them upset.'

I was utterly gutted. There was a lump in my throat. I wanted to cry. But somehow I held back the tears.

I took hold of my huge, heavy suitcase and walked out the front door. It had no wheels so I had to lug it down the street as best as I could, with cars rushing past me. It couldn't have been more humiliating.

All I could do was pray, crying out to the unknown God to send help.

Just as I struggled round a bend in the road, I heard a car pulling up beside me.

It was my boss and she was in tears.

'I'll give you a lift to the station,' she said.

At first I didn't want to get in the car. I was furious with her. But the cold was beginning to bite and I had just prayed for help so that didn't seem very wise.

'I'm sorry,' she stuttered.

But I was speechless.

When we pulled up at the station she thrust some money in my hand, just enough for a meal and a rail ticket.

As she drove away, I stood by the road next to the station as happy people wandered by, doing their shopping, holding hands, laughing.

I couldn't believe what had happened. I knew that giving my notice would have been inconvenient, but I never expected them to cast me out in just a couple of days.

The streets of the picturesque little town now seemed cold and heartless. Everyone was in the holiday spirit, buying champagne for the night's celebrations.

But I wasn't invited.

And they didn't either notice or care.

I boarded the train for Manhattan, bearing my suitcase full of all my worldly possessions. I managed to get a seat among drunken revellers, one of whom noticed my melancholy face.

'Smile,' he said. 'What's the worst that could happen?'

But the worst had happened.

It was New Year's Eve 1987 and I was officially homeless – on my way to the icy streets of New York City.

13

Cold Streets and Candy Treats

Angels often seem to travel in disguise.

I was on my way to the Big Apple by train and it looked as if I was going to spend the night homeless. As I sat in a state of desperation I let out a sigh. At that moment a lady in a red beret came and sat opposite me. At first she just read her book. While she did I was praying to the unknown God for help. Within seconds she caught my eye and started speaking to me. I didn't quite hear what she said but I realized from her accent that she was Irish, so I started chatting with her.

Before long I was telling her my story.

'I've been fired from my job as a nanny and thrown out of the house on New Year's Eve. I have nowhere to go. I'm really in trouble.'

The woman in the red beret looked at me and smiled.

'Well, you can stay in my apartment if you want. You can sleep on the pull-out sofa. My roommate is away tonight.'

I couldn't believe it.

'Thank God, I have somewhere warm to sleep,' I said under my breath.

That night I found myself in an apartment in Upper Manhattan. It was tiny, cramped and not very clean, but I didn't care. I was warm. It was dry. Thanks to an Irish angel in a red beret, I had somewhere to sleep.

The next day I had to go back onto the streets to find accommodation. So off I went with my suitcase. I began to ask strangers passing by if they knew where the YMCA was. It seemed like a good idea to try to find a room there, but no one seemed to know where it was.

My suitcase was now becoming intolerably heavy, like the great sadness I felt in my heart.

I didn't dare leave my case on the sidewalk. It was all I had left to my name.

I was cold and in a daze and I was now becoming afraid. I stood on the corner of a bustling Avenue and just stared. Wild thoughts swirled around my head like snowflakes in an icy gale. I entertained desperate notions of becoming an escort girl or a Mafia assassin – anything to earn enough money to have somewhere warm to live, some food to eat.

I was losing touch with reality.

Then, all of a sudden, I felt what I can only describe as a Presence around me. It was like a bubble and it was moving, and I was moving with it – perhaps even being moved *by* it. It steered me towards a payphone. I entered the phone box and started to dial someone whose name and number I had been given by my sister before I left the UK all those months ago. It was the number of an exchange buddy of a friend of hers who lived in Long Island. I had rung it a few times in the previous months, but had never managed to talk to anyone.

I heard the sound of the ringtone.

'Hello,' I heard a male voice say.

'Hello, I'm Deborah. My sister gave me your number. You know a friend of hers really well.'

'Oh, hi Deborah, we've been trying to get in touch with you for a while. This is my parents' telephone number. We've been picking up your messages, but usually several days after you've left them. We didn't have a number to return your calls.'

'Oh, I'm sorry.'

'My wife and I have been sending you letters, but we didn't get a reply so we figured you were fine.'

'I wish I was,' I replied.

'Are you OK?'

Over the next minute or so I shared what had happened to me, holding back the tears.

'Listen,' he said, 'I want you to get on a train straight away. You come and stay with my wife and me in Patchogue, Long Island. I'll explain which train station you need in Manhattan and which train you have to get. I'll meet you at our local station.'

'I don't know what to say,' I stammered. 'I don't know what I'd have done if you hadn't answered.'

'That's the odd thing,' the man said. 'It's pure chance that my wife and I were here at my parents' house today. And it's strange that I answered the phone. Usually I don't bother because it's always for them.'

'Well, I want to thank you,' I said.

And in my heart I said a silent thank you to the one who was watching over me that night, the one who had intervened on my behalf to spare me sleeping on the freezing streets of New York City.

And so it was I found myself on a train bound for Long Island, uttering a massive sigh of relief. I didn't know what this guy and his wife were like, but if he was a friend of my sister's friend, the chances were they were kind people.

When I alighted from the train I spotted my rescuer.

He came towards me and gave me a big hug.

I burst into tears.

'It's going to be OK,' he said. 'Any friend of my friends is always welcome.'

As we drove to their house, he turned to me.

'We'll gladly help you if you help us with a small matter,' he said.

'Name it.'

'We're in desperate need of a nanny so that my wife can go back to full-time work. It's been a struggle financially, surviving on one income. Will you help in exchange for meals and a place to stay, just until you find a job?'

'Of course I will.'

For the next three or four weeks I stayed at their house and looked after their little boy while they both went out to work. The deal was that I would lodge with them until I found a proper, paid job, and I was to search for one while I was looking after their son. The idea of becoming an escort girl or an assassin had thankfully died a natural death, and so I started buying the papers and applying for a few jobs as a nanny.

I wasn't with them for long but in that time I met their friends and wider family and even went to a wedding. They were part of a big family and they were all very close so the wedding was really enjoyable. Many of the family members were Italians and they were very friendly and generous.

Everyone wanted to hear what I had to say and I was given a lot to eat and drink. There were also some very handsome Italian men there with dark hair and light blue eyes – my favourite. I was enjoying myself!

In fact, I was *really* enjoying myself.

At one point, I relaxed so much that I decided to humble one of the guests at the circular table where I was sitting. He was opposite me. To me and others it seemed as if he was rather too full of himself, so I secretly placed some dessert on my spoon and launched it at him. It was like slow motion. The delicious cake went through the air and landed smack bang in the middle of the guy's expensive silk tie.

He hit the roof!

What happened next was like a scene from *The Godfather*.

There were shouts, curses and threats such as:

'I'm gonna kill da person who did this!'

'You're a dead man!'

He threw his chair back and continued breathing fire, causing the entire room to fall silent – all except for me and the two people either side who'd stared in disbelief as I had prepared the missile. They and I could not stop snorting with laughter, trying, with a great lack of success, to suppress our convulsions.

Eventually those around the man helped him to calm down and normality was restored. But the three of us who had been in on the antic excused ourselves, left the room and found relief outside.

'He had it coming,' one of them said.

'Yeah, but he's not a man to mess with,' the other said soberly.

We laughed anyway and then went back to the party.

After the wedding I started to think about why I had enjoyed it all so much. The people I had met and who had taken me to their hearts seemed genuine, and they were clearly big believers in family values. They also seemed to take their faith seriously. I don't know how committed they were, but there were crosses and pictures of Jesus dotted around their home. One of them in particular used to hold my attention. It was as if Jesus was staring directly at me every time I looked at it.

They clearly loved fun as well. At weekends, the couple had a ritual which they referred to as their 'candy treat'. At first I thought this referred to sweets, but I soon discovered that they were in fact referring to snorting cocaine.

I had not seen cocaine before. I had once experimented with speed a few years before. I also drank alcohol like most people did. But this stuff was new to me.

When my hostess offered some to me, I thought, *Why not? I'll give it a try.*

No one had ever talked to me about cocaine, especially its dangers, so I went along with it.

She put some cocaine on the dresser in her bedroom. She produced a small mountain of chalky powder which she then proceeded to chop with the edge of her credit card into long white lines.

She then showed me how to roll up a dollar bill and insert one end in one nostril, close the other nostril, and snort the cocaine using the banknote as a kind of straw.

She was so excited about it that I got excited too, and every time she went into the bedroom to snort a line, I did too.

That night I partied with a group of friends until very late – drinking, snorting, watching TV, chatting and playing games.

It was after 4 a.m. when I suddenly became aware that I could no longer speak. My jaw was clamped shut. The muscles on both sides of my face were rigid and my heart was beating at a million miles per hour. As I looked around the room I could see that everyone was asking me questions but I couldn't answer.

I thought I was going to die.

I finally managed to communicate that I was in trouble and everyone started to panic, swearing at my hostess for giving me too much cocaine. But I didn't blame her. I was the one following her into the bedroom and I was the one choosing to take the drug.

In retrospect, given that it was my first time, someone should have warned me of the dangers or watched over me. I was extremely lucky that I didn't overdose. In any event, I spent forty-eight hours wide awake on the sofa bed with my jaw fixed and my life flashing before my eyes.

It was no joke.

I really felt I was on the point of death.

In my heart I pleaded with the unknown God watching over me, whom I sensed was not happy.

Spare my life, please. I'm really sorry for pushing it too far. Forgive me.

Eventually I came down and my jaw unlocked.

I fell asleep.

But before I did, I vowed that I would never use cocaine again.

14

The Dark-haired Man

Needless to say, it wasn't long before I was moving again, this time to a family in upstate New York. It also wasn't long before I was beginning to question whether there was more to life than working as a family servant. There had to be more than this. Hadn't that psychic predicted that I would meet and marry a dark-haired man? Well, where was he? Where was my knight in shining armour?

Luckily for me I made a new best friend, and she and I started going out to find fun. She was a glamorous woman with loads of make-up and big permed hair. Often we would work out together or go out for walks. But at other times we went out drinking, driving, clubbing, doing drugs and sleeping around.

I wasn't really happy going from man to man. Deep down, I was looking for Mr Right.

Both of us, in fact, were looking for love.

One night in March 1988, an Irish friend invited me to her birthday party at the Holiday Inn in Mount Kisco. I went somewhat reluctantly because I was beginning to grow tired of being the life and soul of the party. Being tall, at six foot one inches, I could command a room. And when I was high on drugs or alcohol (or both), I became a daredevil, well known for livening up the dullest of parties.

That night, however, I was not in the mood to brighten someone else's birthday. I was craving more intimate company – which, in reality, was my preference anyway. If you had asked me, 'Which do you like better, dinner with one person you really enjoy, or a party with loads of people you don't really know?', I'd have chosen the first any day.

Nevertheless, I decided to go, and that night I walked into the bar area of the Holiday Inn. The room had an oval-shaped bar in the centre. As I reached the group of friends, I was bought a drink and I began to warm to the occasion.

As the evening progressed, a blond guy sitting the opposite side of the room started to buy me drinks. He wasn't my type at all, but I wasn't going to refuse free drinks and so I accepted.

We then started writing notes to each other on our napkins and sending them via an amused barman, who became our unofficial go-between. He was then joined by a dark-haired man who started reading the notes and laughing with the blond guy at what we were writing.

When I found out that the dark-haired guy didn't know the other man, I told him off in a note for being nosy. The dark-haired guy replied by writing that he wanted to buy me a drink and come over and have a chat. I said no but he came over anyway, even pursuing me to the dance floor as I tried to get away.

He kept chatting to me and it quickly became clear that he was a good laugh. We stayed up till 4 a.m. at a diner, talking to each other. When we said goodbye he insisted on having my phone number. I liked him but I figured like most guys he would take it but never call. Much to my surprise, he did call and we started dating. It turned out he was a gentleman and a really nice guy. He opened doors for me and made me feel special. He also lived just down the road from me so we were able to see a lot of each other.

The trouble was that I didn't treat him very well. I had been used to Mr Suave but Untrustworthy, or Mr Exciting but Non-Committal. I had never met Mr Nice Guy before, and I wasn't used to someone who was comparatively unexciting and yet dependable and kind. And if I'm honest, after what I'd been through with my dad, I also felt somewhere in my heart that I didn't deserve someone who treated me well. I didn't know how to deal with it.

So to begin with I was not pleasant. I stood him up on many occasions because I had found something more exciting to do. I also forgot some of our dates and didn't show up. But all the while he was patient and forgiving and little by little the relationship became more and more serious until one day he invited me to move in with him and I said yes.

Here was a man who genuinely cared about me and wanted the best for me.

Here was a man that someone had foreseen would come into my life.

It all felt so 'meant to be'.

This feeling increased when I saw his house on the day I moved in with him. It was identical to the picture of a house I had drawn ages ago in England.

That sent shivers up and down my spine.

Our relationship began to blossom. He might not have been the most exciting man I had ever dated but he was handsome, kind and funny, and he did have a wild side. In fact he was taking drugs. One day I confronted him about this. I told him he had a choice – the coke or me.

He chose me.

After that our love for each other deepened until one day he popped the question.

He lived on another man's horse farm and maintained the property for him. He had asked his boss if it was all right for me to move in. His boss was old-fashioned so he said that he was OK with that but that he'd be happier if we got married first, because that was the traditional thing to do. We had ignored this at the time, but after I moved in, his boss asked what our plans were and it became clear that this was an important issue for him. For me it was the first time I'd ever had anyone suggest to me that it was more appropriate to be married than just living together.

Moving in to his house had, of course, meant moving out of someone else's – the boss's where I worked as a nanny. She was none too pleased and let me have it, threatening me with all sorts. It was an extremely tense moment, but in the midst of all the turbulence suddenly I heard my nan's voice.

'It's all going to be OK,' she said.

That night I told my boyfriend what I had heard.

We were spooning in bed at the time.

After he heard Nan's words, he held onto me and ever so casually proposed to me. I don't know that either of us was ready to take that step, but it seemed so right. I knew he loved me. So I said yes.

The proposal was hardly romantic.

But it seemed practical.

So now I was engaged and there was a wedding to prepare.

We set the day for my birthday – 20 November of the same year (1988). This was not far away. In fact, the preparations were rushed and the actual event felt last-minute. Sadly it all happened so quickly that none of my family from the UK were able to make it. In the end it was a low-key event. My fiancé had been married before and his first wedding had been a big church event. He didn't want the same again.

When the day came it was hard not to be a little disappointed. It was tipping down with rain and there weren't many people there – us, my bridesmaid, his best man and a few friends. None of his family were there either.

I wore a dress that my Irish friend had given me. It was at her birthday party that my fiancé and I had met and exchanged notes across the bar. I had a garter bought for me and flowers given to me. I did my own hair and make-up and my best friend drove me to the Italian restaurant where we were married by a Justice of the Peace.

The reception – such as it was – felt more like a birthday party than a wedding. Since it was my birthday, someone had organized for the restaurant to make a birthday cake with candles instead of a wedding cake.

This was obviously the cause of quite a lot of curiosity.

Indeed, a lady who was dining at another table in the restaurant came over to ours.

'I'm confused,' she said. 'Is this a wedding or a birthday?'

'It's both,' I said.

'Ah,' she replied, 'in that case, *mazel tov*!'

She bought us a bottle of champagne to celebrate and then went back to her seat.

After no time at all, our guests had to leave and my husband and I returned to normality. It had all been so surreal that it almost felt as if the wedding had never happened.

However, one sure sign that it had happened was the fact that I was now married to a US citizen and therefore able to get a job legally.

So I went from working illegally as a nanny to working legally in Macy's for Clarins. This meant that I was back to my first love – beauty therapy.

In no time at all, I felt much better about life. I was using my hard-earned qualifications at last and I was working in the field I loved.

There were challenges. Being behind a cosmetics counter could be boring and it didn't always feel comfortable forcing products on customers. But I liked the store, and selling cosmetics was far better than being a nanny.

Even though it still felt as though there was more to life than selling cosmetics, the dark-haired man I had been promised had arrived on the scene.

Maybe things were, at last, looking up for me.

15

A Gathering of Angels

My marriage coincided with a new quest for the spiritual dimension to life. I found a New Age crystal store and spent a lot of time there, getting to know the staff and reading books by authors such as Brian Weiss, Shirley MacLaine and Nancy Friday. I studied a lot about the 11:11 movement which was big in the early 1990s, and listened to whatever tapes I could find. I consulted with astrologers and psychics, made my own runes and bought a variety of tarot cards. I attended shaman sessions and past-life regression sessions. I tried Buddhism, chanting 'Om mani padme hum', and visited an ashram. I went on spiritual retreats and attended meetings. I used crystals and a Ouija board, gazed into crystal balls and went digging for garnets and quartz. I tried 'channelling' and automatic writing. In the end, I was in the New Age crystal store so often that the manager gave me a job there.

Many of those I met during this time were lovely, open individuals who were on a similar quest for spiritual knowledge and enlightenment. All of us were trying to make sense of our existence and looking wherever we could for answers. I can only remember a few who seemed to me to have an aura of darkness around them.

My spiritual quest became so intense during this phase that at one point I even looked into witchcraft, but aside from meeting a few white witches and trying out a few spells I didn't get very far. Something or someone held me back from becoming too involved, and in the end it was a convent not a coven that attracted me.

One day I decided to go to a convent with a friend from the store. While we were there she wanted to go into the convent shop. She had been brought up a Catholic so she was interested in what they had there.

I remember being drawn to the crucifixes although I didn't buy one. Later, as my friend and I strolled around the convent grounds, we came to a hill overlooking a lake. A cross had been planted on the top and we walked around it before sitting down to enjoy the view.

Before we left, I heard a voice in my heart saying, 'Look down!'

The voice took me by surprise, but I obeyed and dropped my gaze to my feet.

Where there had been only dirt and a bit of grass before, now there was a handmade rosary.

'Where did that come from?' I asked, pointing to the rosary.

'I don't know,' my friend replied, 'but it definitely wasn't there when I walked over that spot a few moments ago.'

'What do you think it means?'

'I don't know,' she replied, 'but it's given me the chills.'

'I just feel peace,' I said, as I took the rosary in my hands and pocketed it.

I still have that today.

It will be no surprise to learn that during this season I referred to myself as a 'spiritual seeker'. As you know by now, I had always been aware of someone watching over me and the incident with the rosary made me wonder whether this was some kind of sign from the unknown God. That in turn added fuel to my desire to seek after truth wherever I could find it and to experience the spiritual and mystical realm as often as I could.

It was about this time that I began to have some interesting out-of-body experiences. These took the same form – floating in my spirit above a location, seeing things, relating these observations to someone else, and them confirming that what I had seen in my out-of-body state was real.

The first time this happened I was lifted up in my spirit over our house and saw some things which I then described to my husband and which he confirmed.

Another time we were camping, having decided to dig for quartz. During the night some people arrived next to us on the site. I was lifted up in my spirit above my tent and saw the people arrive and noted what they looked like. In the morning I woke up and the people next door had already left. I told my husband what I had observed. He had been up much earlier and seen them. He confirmed that this was exactly how the people looked. He was amazed by how accurate all the details were because he knew that I had been zipped up inside the tent and had not left it all night.

However, this didn't mean my husband shared my interest in spiritual phenomena. In fact, he didn't seem to have a spiritual bone in his body. The only hint of any spirituality was when he went hunting. He would pray to his forefathers during the hunting season for 'a big buck'. Otherwise we were travelling different paths. He was into shooting and fishing and I was into crystals and runes.

As these paths diverged, two other paths reunited. I am referring here to my relationship with my dad, which had broken down as a result of the divorce and abandonment. I had begun to do some informal study of psychology, especially into the effects that a woman's relationship with her dad has on her relationships with men. I realized that the lack of a father's love had scarred me deeply.

I looked into therapy around this time because I knew that I needed help with my father-wounds. I also knew that the only way forward was to forgive my dad; otherwise my hurts would continue to obstruct true intimacy in my relationships with men. I was especially keen that my own emotional baggage wouldn't adversely affect my marriage.

With that in mind, I decided to contact Dad with a view to reconciling with him. My dad had not tried to get in touch with me, to find me or get to know me since leaving us that fateful day he had called at our house in Somerton from Kuwait. So I knew there was a risk of further rejection. But I persisted anyway. Not only was I spiritually thirsty, I was also suffering from a deep father hunger.

It was through my sister that I discovered how to find Dad. I wrote some letters to him and then we had a very emotional reunion. As soon as I forgave him for the hurts he had caused me as a child I felt free. It was as if a great weight had been lifted from both of us and consequently a new relationship was forged between us. It was a little challenging at first because he was living in Ireland and I was in America, the time difference didn't help when it came to calling him on the phone. But the journey to healing had begun and I was excited by that.

My spiritual journey was gathering pace too, and I started a guided meditation group called 'A Gathering of Angels'. This was for spiritual guidance and support. I knew that angels existed because I'd always had a sense that I was being watched and cared for by someone or something invisible. As I started the group I was thrilled to find people who shared my beliefs.

The Gathering of Angels would meet at my house or, on the odd occasion, at one of the other members' houses. I suggested we all wear white. I had no real idea why I felt that way except that it seemed to symbolize purity and light.

I remembered my confession as a 10-year-old that day back in Kuwait in front of my Barbie doll's house when I had said I wanted to wear only white linen, cotton or silk – that I wanted to be pure.

It felt as though something was coming full circle.

Then, one day, something extraordinary occurred in the group. I was guiding the members through a meditation and encouraging them to visualize what I was describing. I am a very visual person with a rich dream life and an equally rich imagination, so visualization was easy for me. I began to describe what I was seeing to the group.

'Let me take you on a journey,' I said. 'You are in a garden and slightly to your right is an archway covered in beautiful roses.'

I paused.

'Just beyond the archway a very bright light is radiating. It is a brilliant, white light.'

I paused again, allowing my listeners to see what I was seeing and to drink in the moment.

During the silence I began to see something. There was a figure coming towards me.

'There is a man approaching under the arch,' I said, 'and he is surrounded by an immense amount of light.'

I paused again.

The group waited.

But I couldn't say any more.

I was utterly overwhelmed by the man's magnificence, struck dumb by his majesty.

Tears streamed down my face.

All I eventually could do was stutter: 'There is a . . . very important being . . . in this room . . . and we are just . . . to be . . . in his presence . . .'

I knew who it was. It was Jesus. But I simply couldn't get his name out of my mouth. That was not unusual for me. I had visited my friend's church a couple of times and had even come across a Bible. But for some obscure reason I had never been able to utter the name 'Jesus'.

As he walked closer to me, the light of his glory was dazzling.

To my right I saw a well. He walked over to it and then beckoned to me to come and sit with him. In my mind I walked over to him and he started to speak to me. But I couldn't hear what he was saying. All I could do was cry quietly as I watched him stir the water with his left hand.

I don't know how long it was before the vision began to fade and I eventually closed the session but a few of the members had described feeling an amazing presence.

All of us went home quietly that day, feeling stunned.

In our Gathering of Angels, it seemed as if we had met with someone who was more than an angel.

16

Special Hands

Given the deteriorating state of my marriage, it was perhaps not the best idea to set off as a couple to the Grand Canyon. Things were rocky enough already. But in an attempt to bond with my husband and broaden our horizons, we went on a road trip through the Rocky Mountains in Colorado, then Arizona and on to Utah. My hope was that we would draw closer in the great outdoors, especially on a spiritual level. But in the end when we finally got to Sedona in Arizona all he wanted was to stay in the hotel and drink beer and I wanted to go out on a shaman's walk. He didn't mind me going so I went, but what I'd really wanted was for him to join me.

As it turned out, the lady who walked with me wasn't very helpful. I already knew that my relationship needed a lot of work. But then she told me that I wasn't in the right marriage. The walk in the desert was therefore not altogether constructive. Apart from one thing, that is: everywhere I went I saw crosses in the dirt and even in the rocks. I didn't know what this signified but it did give me a feeling of spiritual elation.

This feeling increased a few days later while visiting the Chapel of the Holy Cross in Sedona. On entering I sensed something that I'd never experienced before – as if someone was calling out to me, whispering my name from the end of a long tunnel.

When we got home I continued my spiritual search. I had not found what I'd been looking for spiritually or emotionally on the trip, in spite of a Sunrise Ceremony in which I felt very connected to the Creator, and a helicopter ride in the Grand Canyon in which I marvelled at the beautiful diversity of creation.

I had enjoyed the journey but I certainly didn't feel as if I had arrived.

One day, however, a Japanese lady came into the New Age crystal store where I was working.

'I would like to invite you to my house tonight,' she said after we had chatted for a few minutes about Reiki healing.

'That's kind,' I replied.

'You should start training this evening as a Reiki healer.'

'Do you think so?'

'Yes,' the lady replied, 'you have very special hands.'

That night I went to the lady's house in Greenwich, Connecticut, and had my initiation into phase one of my training to become a Reiki master. The lady then told me I needed to practice for the next two years until I was ready for phase two. The extraordinary thing is that two years later I was in another New Age store, this time in Ridgefield, Connecticut, and I bumped into a woman who out of the blue declared, 'You're ready for phase two of Reiki healing.'

What a coincidence!

I took the woman's details, went to her house and started the training.

However, on both occasions (starting phase one and starting phase two) I had a feeling of discomfort in my spirit. I knew that something wasn't quite right – especially when the second lady wanted to draw Reiki symbols on my forehead – but I couldn't put my finger on it. No one had ever given me any instruction on discerning what exactly we were 'channelling' – channelling is opening yourself up to allow disembodied spiritual forces to flow through you – I naively went along with it and put my misgivings down to my unresolved issues. After all, I had 'special hands', I seemed willing to allow any old spirit to operate through me without much thought given to the source of that spirit!

Not long after that training in Reiki, I met a lady in her sixties at the gym where I was working as a receptionist. I had finished my job selling cosmetics and now worked at the gym part-time. The lady was a massage therapist and she'd come in that day to work on a client. It was the first time I had met her.

I knew there was more to life than being a receptionist and so I'd been praying to the unknown God – or the Universal Light, to use my preferred phrase at that time – for guidance.

The massage therapist got chatting with me and after a few minutes said, 'Let me see your hands.'

I presented them to her and she inspected them.

'You have special hands,' she said. 'You should be using them.'

'I wish I could,' I replied.

'You should think of becoming a massage therapist,' she replied.

'I've always wanted to do that here,' I cried. 'When I was back in England I qualified as an Aesthetician but when I came out to the States I was prevented from working as a massage therapist because the laws and licensing system over here are different. In any case, I wouldn't know where to start now.'

'May I make a suggestion?' she asked.

'Sure.'

'Why don't you apply to the training school where I've just graduated?'

'Where is that?' I asked.

'It's in Westport, Connecticut.'

'Oh my goodness,' I exclaimed. 'That's near where I live! I never knew there was a massage school there.'

I was so excited. Maybe this was the answer to my prayers!

I couldn't wait to explore the possibilities. I went home and told my husband and he agreed that it was a good idea, so I went to Westport and enrolled in the massage school. I was offered a place straight away. The only problem was that it was very near the start of the course and I had to raise $8,000 very quickly to pay just for the classes. This did not include the cost of all the equipment I was going to need to buy for my work as well.

I went home and talked to my husband.

'I'm afraid the course is very expensive.'

'How much is it?' he asked.

'It's eight grand, and that doesn't include what I'll need to pay on equipment.'

'That's a lot of money.'

'I know.'

'Well, you're going to have to fund it yourself. I can't help you.'

I was stuck. How on earth was I going to raise that kind of money as a part-time receptionist?

Being a fighter, I didn't give up. The next day I phoned the school and explained my predicament.

'Don't let that deter you,' the person said. 'You can always apply for student loans. You're eligible.'

I was amazed.

I filled in the extremely complicated paperwork and managed to start the course. As I did, I noticed a change in my husband's attitude. Suddenly he wasn't so keen. It seemed to me that he'd originally been supportive because he thought the idea was a non-starter. Now that I had begun at the massage school, his backing waned. It seemed that we were growing even further apart, and that was killing me inside.

However, I put all that to the back of my mind and began my classes at the school. If I was going to be a massage therapist in the States I was going to need the training. The US didn't recognize my UK qualifications so I had to start again if I was going to be a licensed practitioner. I wanted to run my own business and I realized that I had to go back to school to do that.

As it happened, running a business didn't seem such an unattainable idea. There were new owners at the farm where we lived and they had purchased the adjoining house. They gave us this new house to live in. It was much bigger than our previous one – three bedrooms, three bathrooms, a formal dining room, large garden and so on. Looking at it I felt I could easily run a business there.

The only obstacle was my husband. He was becoming more and more antagonistic and obviously feeling more and more threatened, especially when I was in the company of other men. I was desperate to reassure him and even more desperate to see our marital problems resolved. I suggested we went to counselling together but he wouldn't go. I loved him dearly but we were travelling in different directions.

To make matters worse, my spiritual advisors were telling me I was in the wrong marriage.

And to make things even more complicated, other men started giving me the affirmation and attention that my husband wasn't. It was all a recipe for disaster – a disaster which was now inevitable.

For the time being, however, I found purpose and solace in my training. While I was still at the school I began the process of setting up my own massage therapy business, though not in our new house at the farm. I asked the unknown God what I should call it. I sensed I should give it the name 'Heartfelt Touch'. I had seen a picture in my mind of both my hands in the shape of a heart so I turned that into the company logo. I wrote the name up on the whiteboard in my classroom at the school and to my astonishment it remained there for weeks. Nobody seemed to want to erase it!

For the first time I felt truly energized and motivated. I was running a business doing something I loved and in a field where I felt truly at home.

First impressions are crucial, so I made sure that I bought the very best massage table and top-quality cotton sheets, and one of the best makes of dual-purpose massage cream. I took great pride in my appearance and made sure that I looked my very best, and that standards of hygiene were above and beyond reproach.

Every time clients came for a massage, I would prepare myself spiritually so that I could channel 'love and light' to them through my hands. When I centred myself like this, I could feel heat going through my hands as I massaged them. Many of my clients commented that they felt it too.

Even though there were cynics who insultingly joked that a massage business was a cover for prostitution, I persevered and the business began to grow and I began to prosper, even before I graduated.

For me, I was an agent of healing to my clients. That was my focus. That was my passion.

My dream was to give them a heartfelt touch.

And my clients respected me.

They recommended me to their friends, and before long I had a growing reputation for my special hands.

It was just as the psychic had predicted, all those years ago in England.

17

Broken Hearts

While my hands were hot, my marriage was not.

Don't get me wrong, I loved my husband and wanted so badly for things to work out with us. But we had drifted far apart and were travelling on different paths. Every attempt to try to bring our paths into some kind of convergence seemed to fail dismally. In spite of our best efforts, it just wasn't working, and the tension between us was escalating. If he wasn't working he was off pursuing one of his hobbies, and I frequently found myself alone.

Things became so stressful that I decided I had to have a break. I felt I just needed to get away and clear my head. A week would do, preferably by the sea, in a place where I could reflect about the past and plan for the future.

As it happened, this wish was fulfilled quickly.

I had a friend at the gym where I worked. She was one of my best friends and she felt the same way about needing some space. She was a personal trainer. A couple of days after we talked, a client of hers came into the gym. He mentioned to her that he was building a hotel on St Thomas, a beautiful island in the Caribbean, one of the US Virgin Islands, and that the house next to it was going to be empty for a week.

It was where the construction workers lived while building the hotel.

'Would you like to have the house for a week while they're away?' he asked. 'You can stay there for free.'

Needless to say we accepted the offer and I went home and told my husband about it. After reassurances that I was going with a girlfriend, not a man, he said I could go and off I went. Within days my friend and I were in a soft-top jeep driving from the airport under a blazing sun and between palm trees. As we drove near the bright blue sea, I could feel the tension lift from my shoulders.

We arrived at the large double gates to the house, full of anticipation. When they opened we screamed with excitement. The gates had already suggested that this was no ordinary place, but when we arrived it was beyond our dreams. We had the keys to a six-bedroom villa with six bathrooms. Furthermore, there was a swimming pool which had a view over the bay.

We jumped out of the jeep, chose our rooms and then settled down with a cocktail. As the sun set, we gave a toast and started to unwind.

Over the next few days we toured the island. We took long walks on the white sandy beaches where the tropical fish swam close to the shore. We swam in the sea, which was crystal clear with a tint of turquoise. We sunbathed and drank cocktails, went to restaurants and ate seafood. We took the ferry to Tortola where we attended the Full Moon party at Bomba Shack. A few days later we went by ferry to St John's which was so beautiful I cried. It was perfect.

In times of quiet, I thought about my marriage. I was gutted at the thought that history was repeating itself – both my parents and my husband's parents had divorced. To make matters worse, my husband's first wife had left him for another man. I really didn't want it to happen again. I had been the 'fixer' when I had to support my mother. Surely I could fix my own relationship.

By the end of my idyllic break I had made up my mind. I was going to give it one more go. Before the holiday I had challenged my husband to find a therapist he liked since he never liked any of the therapists I had chosen. Maybe – just maybe – he had found one who could help us. Maybe there was a chance that we could stop the rot and begin to grow a healthy marriage.

We left St Thomas's a few days later, having said goodbye to the villa we'd been staying in. Even as we touched down at the airport back home I felt the heavy weight of frustration and apprehension returning to my shoulders. But when I walked through my front door, I found to my surprise that my husband had indeed signed up with a therapist – so off we went.

It was a disaster.

My husband had already had a session without me and provided a litany of grievances against me. The therapist barely allowed me to tell my side of the story. He just tore into me, reducing me to tears. Even my husband was embarrassed by the intensity of the counsellor's tirade. He apologized afterwards, but the damage had been done. We never went again and I lost the energy to fix the unfixable.

Once again I immersed myself in my training and the business I had built. I loved both, and before long I graduated. I was even asked to give a speech at the graduation ceremony.

My husband didn't show up to listen.

That hurt.

By the end of 1995, I had moved into the spare bedroom. It had been a long time since we had enjoyed sexual intimacy. That had been a source of immense grief to me. For me, making love was the closest thing to a spiritual connection with my husband.

I had two one-night stands with different men in the subsequent weeks. I'm not proud of it. Neither of them meant anything and I never saw them again. Both times I had been drunk. That hadn't helped. When I had sobered up, on both occasions I felt terrible. I cried in the shower, but I couldn't wash my shame away.

Shortly after my thirtieth birthday, I suggested we should separate. My husband, who never got angry, flew into a rage and shouted that if I walked out the door he would divorce me. That was not the reaction I was either expecting or wanting. What I really needed was him to hold me tight and tell me that we would sort it out. I only suggested separation because I thought we needed the space. But it seemed as if now we were headed for more than that.

What I didn't realize at the time was the depth of the damage caused by some of my spiritual practices. Seeing psychics had not helped. The most recent one had told me that I should leave my husband. Looking back, I now see that the advice of these people, and the spiritual root of that advice, caused carnage. I can't blame my broken marriage on that. I made poor choices and so did my husband. At the same time, there were destructive spiritual forces at work.

And so I chose to pack and leave. That process was not easy because my husband kept inspecting my belongings to see if I was taking anything that he deemed his. In the end I let him have all the furniture. I just took my clothes, possessions and a few household items.

Leaving the farm was awful. It was the longest I had ever stayed in the same place in my entire life. We had been married for seven years and I had come to love our home. Saying goodbye to my 'baby' – the beautiful dog we'd adopted – was one of the worst moments of my life. He needed to stay on the farm where there was more room to roam. I was going to stay with a girlfriend and it wouldn't have been fair to have him cooped up there.

It was time to accept that a chapter was ending and that things were about to change. But the transition was horrible. I went from living in a big house with freedom to do what I liked to living in a guest room in a friend's house with few of those options.

To make ends meet, I had to take on another job in addition to my massage work, so back I went to being a nanny, and I also did some house-sitting and pet-sitting.

Six months later, in June 1996, I found myself in a lawyer's office. My husband was there too. The period of separation had come to an end and it was now time for closure.

We signed the divorce papers.

We were both in tears.

He said he regretted divorcing me, but that it was too late.

Driving away from the lawyer's office I felt numb. I couldn't believe everything had happened so quickly. In a strange way I felt free, but I was also dead inside.

I was now a divorcee.

We had got married on my birthday.

When the divorce papers arrived, it was on his birthday.

And now I was on the move again.

18

Thai Massage School

In the months that followed my divorce I resorted to a familiar anaesthetic. Having sex had always been my main way of coping with emotional pain. Now more than ever I needed that 'fix' if I was to survive the disappointment and devastation of my divorce.

I started to go out with a self-professed Italian stallion, triathlete and skydiver. I went skydiving a couple of times with him. During the second time I remember hearing a voice saying, 'Thou shalt not tempt the Lord thy God!' I remember thinking, 'Where the heck did that come from?' I never went skydiving again. I also ditched the skydiver. He was good-looking and had a great physique, but our intimacy was mechanical and loveless. There was no spiritual connection with him. I missed love.

Towards the end of the year I decided that I needed to get away. I had moved house so many times and had nowhere to call home. Clients had been hard to come by too; being a self-employed business owner really is like riding a rollercoaster – one minute you're up, the next you're down. I was looking for direction, big-time.

During the year I had been introduced to Swami Muktananda's ashram; it was now headed by a woman called Gurumayi Chidvilasananda. The New Age group I had met were planning to go to St John's Island, which I had previously visited and loved. They planned to do meditation, yoga and past-life regression.

I signed up to go, but before heading there I had already decided to go to Thailand with a friend from the massage school. He and I wanted to learn Thai massage in a training centre in Chiang Mai. So I thought it would do me good to head to Bangkok and do the training in Chiang Mai, before joining the group from the ashram for the retreat on St John's Island. It would be a much needed and timely distraction, and I'd have time to do a lot of sightseeing.

However, I wasn't as prepared as perhaps I should have been when I flew to Thailand. The house where I was staying at the time in Westport was in uproar, with the couple I was living with talking about separating. I had booked my tickets through a newspaper advert, but in all the chaos of my domestic situation I had forgotten to arrange a place to meet my friend.

When I realized this, I hoped in my heart that I would find once again that the unknown God of the universe would be watching over me and that I would be all right.

I arrived in Bangkok and took a taxi, asking the driver to find me a cheap hotel in town. He took me to a place in an area of the city where lots of backpackers stayed, and I checked in. The room was grim and tiny. There was a single plastic mattress on a rickety bed.

After a fitful night's sleep, I went out to explore the city. There were temples everywhere and I went to see the biggest golden Buddha I had ever seen, lying on its side in Wat Pho. The pace was frenetic and the atmosphere crazy, yet everyone seemed to be talking about peace and Zen-like calm.

Just as I had been in India as a girl, I was overwhelmed by the contrast between the ornate, opulent temples and the shacks in which the poor were living. There were beggars scavenging everywhere on the streets, along with stray dogs. Poor people and sick people sat with hopeless stares while monks walked past the dying, ignoring them because it was their *karma* – their destiny.

Why couldn't their Buddha help them?

By the next morning, I realized that I really needed to meet up with my friend. I was alone and vulnerable in a strange city and I really wanted his company. But how was I to know where he was? I was starting to panic.

I left the hotel to look for somewhere to eat and have a coffee. I felt drawn to a certain café and sat down with my back to the street.

'Deborah, is that you?'

I turned round and there he was! My friend was emerging from the crowd.

'I thought it was you,' he said, excitedly. 'I spotted you halfway down the street. I could see your bum-length, wavy blonde hair hanging loose! I don't know anyone else with hair like yours.'

With that we laughed and hugged.

'I'm so relieved to see you,' I said.

'You should have contacted me before leaving the US,' he said. 'I had no idea where you were.'

'I'm sorry,' I replied.

'That's OK. We're here now.'

'I'm excited about the training at Chiang Mai.'

'Me too,' he said. 'I'm looking forward to learning Thai massage.'

The next day we took the train to Chiang Mai. We eventually found the group we were supposed to join, but the facilities were awful. There was filthy water next to the room where I was staying and the mosquitoes were big – darn big. I'm an adaptable girl, but I certainly wasn't feeling the Zen at that point!

The following day, we all took a train north. I hadn't realized that we would be travelling further to a remote village for our training. Once we were off the train we then boarded jeeps and drove into the mountains to the village where the massage training school was located.

The main trainer and the founder of the school was a German man who had married a local woman. They had set up their home and the school in the hills. My accommodation was very basic, but fun. I stayed with several other girls in a large hut built on stilts. At dawn, we went to a flattened clearing at the top of one of the hills to practice yoga and meditation before the day's classes began. Getting up early was mandatory, not optional, and there was no coffee in the village to help me wake up. I soon developed dreadful headaches from my caffeine withdrawal.

'Caffeine is poison,' my teacher said. 'You'll just have to bear with it. Here, this might help.'

He proceeded to place my head in a vice-like grip. 'This will alleviate the pain.'

Aside from the temporary relief caused by the immense pressure on my temples, I can safely say it didn't help me one little bit. I continued to suffer, and this did not aid my concentration in class.

The teacher then resorted to a horrendous herbal concoction. It was utterly disgusting and I had to drink it twice a day. Eventually I got so sick I thought I had been poisoned. I threw the rest away, but pretended I was still taking it. In the end I was cured by the merciful intervention of a villager who saw my plight and smuggled in some coffee for me. A few of the other girls were suffering from the same problem so we hid round the back of one of the huts and shared the contraband. We laughed hysterically at our lack of spiritual commitment. After a few cups, however, I began to feel like my old self again, and was able to focus with a clear head on my massage training.

My stay there coincided with the Chinese New Year. During the celebrations I witnessed a two-day slaughtering of pigs. It was awful. I was a vegetarian at the time and the appalling screams of the dying animals assaulted and offended my senses. I couldn't stand it. This was supposed to be a quiet retreat. Now all I could hear were these poor creatures having their throats cut. It felt at odds with what I was being taught, and I was horrified when I learnt that some of the meat was even going to be offered to the local deities.

When it was time to pack and go, I was more than ready. I was relieved to be heading south to Chiang Mai. When we arrived there I settled into a nice hotel, had a few cold beers and some decent food in a restaurant. I had been up in the mountains in a rarefied spiritual atmosphere. I needed to get grounded again.

Back in Bangkok I realized to my horror that my return ticket to the USA was standby only. I managed to board a flight as far as Hong Kong, but then was asked to disembark. The grumpy clerk at the check-in desk couldn't tell me when I could board another flight to the USA because it was the Chinese New Year and the flights were packed. So I was stranded in Hong Kong until further notice, down to my last few dollars, only able to afford rice and yes, you guessed it, coffee.

I slept in my sleeping bag on the floor with my passport tucked under my head for fear of having it stolen. I had phoned my friend in Westport back in the USA, but she hadn't been able to do anything to help me. I really was powerless and it seemed yet again that something or someone was trying to rob me of the peace I'd hoped to gain on this trip. That night I went to sleep feeling very hungry and anxious. The security guards kept giving me filthy looks. I was sweating with worry and in desperate need of a shower.

The next morning I went to the clerk again and asked for a flight. I was beginning to panic, so I quietly asked the unknown God of the universe to help me. No sooner had I finished my prayer than an English lady came up behind me and spoke to the clerk.

'Come with me a minute,' she said to me.

She was about my mum's age and I felt safe with her.

'I hope you don't mind,' she said. 'I overheard your request.'

'I don't mind at all,' I replied.

'Well, my husband is a top executive in the airline. He'll get you on a flight.'

I was overwhelmed with gratitude, both to her and the one watching over me.

'You must be hungry,' she said.

After buying me some food she disappeared, but only after firmly telling the clerk at the desk to make sure I got on the flight.

Not long after that I found myself on board a plane and sitting in my allotted seat. I must have been absolutely exhausted because I fell asleep straight away and only woke up when the flight attendant announced that we were landing. The only problem was that we weren't landing in the USA. We were landing in Canada!

I frantically examined my ticket.

Yes, there it was. The destination clearly said Canada. In my exhaustion I hadn't bothered to look. Adrenalin began to pump around my body. What was I going to do? I didn't have enough money to get from Vancouver to New York.

As I sat there I consoled myself with the thought that at least I was the right side of the Pacific now.

The flight attendant began to speak again.

'All passengers that don't have tickets to New York please disembark.'

Suddenly I understood. The plane was heading to New York but was stopping to let off passengers bound for Canada, as well as to refuel.

But my ticket still went only as far as Vancouver.

There was only one thing for it. I prayed silently to the unknown God of the universe to make the flight attendants overlook the fact that I didn't have a ticket for New York. I prayed that I would become invisible, that as they came round they wouldn't see me and I wouldn't be forced to leave the plane.

I pushed fear away and started to sense a feeling of optimism that whoever was watching over me would look after me and that everything would be OK.

Just as the flight attendant got to me there was a loud shout from the front. She turned. The cabin doors shut. She continued counting the passengers but didn't ask to see my ticket.

I breathed a huge sigh of relief. I was going to be OK. I was heading for New York.

By the time I arrived at New York City I was drenched in sweat.

By the time I arrived in Westport, I was exhausted and hungry.

I ate a meal and then collapsed on my bed and slept for twelve hours.

I had learnt something about Thai massage. But I had also learnt something more important – that the unknown God of the universe was truly with me.

19

The Love Boat

Looking back, I know that there were times when my expectations of finding what I was searching for in life were not met.

The trip to St John's Island was one of many examples of this. I had been so looking forward to the past-life regression retreat with Brian Weiss. I had read his books and was longing to meet him. But in the end, although the workshops were interesting, I doubted some of the stories and it didn't quite work out the way I'd hoped.

There were some positives, however. The island was as beautiful as I had remembered when my best friend from the gym and I had visited previously, and I was so grateful to be back. I'd always known I would return here one day. I stayed in one of the permanent tents overlooking the bay. The view was breathtaking. Standing in the sea at night was also spectacular. There was marine phosphorescence everywhere. It was like having the universe around your legs.

And then there was the vision.

It happened during one of the guided meditations into past lives. As we were asked to close our eyes, we were told to see if we had known anyone else in the room from a past life. I saw a man who wasn't physically in the room. He had dark, shoulder-length wavy hair and a long white robe. He also had arresting blue eyes that looked right into me, as if they could burn a hole in my soul.

When I opened my eyes again, he had gone.

But I knew who he was.

I had seen him before, sitting at a well.

It was Jesus.

Returning to Westport I found that my friend's marriage had now broken down and she had moved her stuff – and mine – to a new place where she let me stay too. I was so grateful to her for helping me like this, especially at such a difficult time. But I knew I couldn't stay long. I wanted to travel and I had a special longing to work on a cruise ship. It would be decent money and I'd get to see more of the world.

I applied for a job working for a cruise line and was offered it. A few weeks later I was on my way to the ship docked in Miami. It was 1997 and I was given an eight-month contract which meant sailing around the Caribbean, the Bahamas, Bermuda, Mexico, up the East Coast of the USA, finishing with a transatlantic cruise from the States to England. This was the perfect way to spend my time as I tried to figure out what the next step was going to be after my divorce seven months prior.

I spent the night before I boarded in a dingy motel in Miami. I slept fitfully. I was aware of dark shadows looming in my room. I was acutely aware of a sinister presence in and around the motel. The next day I learnt from my taxi driver that a murder had taken place in the vicinity. It sent shivers down my spine.

These feelings quickly disappeared as I saw the blue cruise ship out of the taxi window. I was excited now. It all reminded me of the old show called *The Love Boat* and I chuckled. But when I boarded it felt as if there were endless corridors, and I had to fight off a sudden feeling of claustrophobia. As I realized that this massive metal container with hundreds of other souls on board was going to be my home for the next eight months, I felt a wave of unexpected anxiety. *What have I got myself into?*

I need not have worried. It wasn't long before I got used to the routine and the maze of corridors. I was determined to make the most of my experience. We visited some stunningly beautiful places. I was one of the oldest crew members on board, at 31. Most of the crew were in the early twenties. But that wasn't going to stop me having fun.

And I did.

I shared my cabin with a crazy girl from Finland who was having an affair with one of the captain's right-hand men. She was wild and fun. There was always a free bottle of vodka as well as caviar in our little fridge. It wasn't always easy to remain sober with such temptations, or those of the crew bar, where a pretty girl rarely had to pay for a drink. I had to try, though. I was doing eight to ten massages every day on the cruise. 'Days at sea' also involved me in cleaning duties and inventories so I couldn't overdo the partying. At the same time, all the fun was helping me to forget the pain of my divorce. I was glad of that.

But this tactic didn't last. I soon began to be haunted by regrets from the past and anxiety about the future. What was I going to do after the eight-month contract? Where was Mr Right? Was I ever going to meet him?

I felt lost, lost at sea.

However, two things lifted me for a while.

The first was a conversation with a client.

In general I would try not to talk to my clients too much when I gave them a massage because I wanted them to really relax and let go. But sometimes they needed to talk; it was a way of letting off steam. I would let the client decide, and I'd adapt according to what they needed – to talk or zone out.

One day a well-known American footballer came in. We had the preliminary chat about what type of massage he liked and what, if any, areas he needed me to focus on. Then I started the treatment.

As I did, I couldn't help feeling that I was about to have a significant conversation with him. There was something about him I couldn't put my finger on (no pun intended!).

During treatment, I would frequently sense things about people and give them what I believed was a psychic piece of information. I'd do this if I felt it was appropriate, and only after finding out if they were open to such things.

I knew there was something special about this man but I couldn't think what, so I diplomatically asked him if he believed in anything spiritual. He said yes. I immediately had an overwhelming feeling that I could tell him anything; I even felt tearful. But I got a grip of myself and spoke.

'I'm very spiritual and I believe that a lot more exists beyond what we see. I'm searching for the truth about our existence and where we're from and why I'm here. What do you believe in?'

'I'm a Christian,' he replied.

I don't remember what he said after that, but I do know that he talked about Jesus.

A few weeks after he and his wife had left the ship, I received a wonderful surprise. They had sent me a Bible. I didn't remember giving him my contact details. He must have gone out of his way to find out, and his wife had even written me a card inside advising me where to start reading – John's gospel in the New Testament.

I was so deeply touched that they had gone to the trouble to do that.

Unfortunately, no matter how hard I tried, I couldn't understand the Bible. They had sent me the old King James Version and for me – and a lot of people – that's like trying to understand Shakespeare! So I stopped reading.

The second thing that happened on the Love Boat was that I found romance again.

It all happened quite quickly.

One night I was at the crew bar when one of the musicians from the band approached me and asked if I'd have a drink with one of the other band members. At the time I had decided I didn't want anything to do with men. I wanted to sort my head out after the divorce. But as I glanced over at this guy I thought he looked rather handsome in his tuxedo – and he had dark hair! I was also flattered to have been asked out by someone's friend. That hadn't happened since school.

My curiosity was aroused. 'Mr Jazzman' was half-Mexican, half-American and very sultry-looking. As soon as we began to talk I sensed a connection. We drank and chatted for hours, then took a walk to the back of the ship where we lay down, gazing at each other under the brilliant stars.

And he kissed me.

It was an exhilarating kiss that sent shivers down my spine.

And yet, a voice inside me told me something wasn't quite right. That this was going to be overly intense as well as a distraction to my spiritual search – and just at the moment when it seemed as if I was on the very edge of discovering what I'd been looking for.

Very quickly our relationship became all-consuming. We spent all our time off together, exploring the exotic locations where the cruise ship docked. I also began to notice his mood swings. He had a short fuse and a quick temper. But I was too far gone. I had fallen in love with 'Mr Jazzman' so I brushed these things off. This time, I thought, I had met the one.

When his contract was close to expiring, I remember feeling sick. How was I going to cope when he left the ship? Much to my surprise, however, he told me that he felt exactly the same way about me, and suggested we should have a break together in the middle of my contract.

'Come to Vegas and help me move to Atlanta,' he said.

He was about to move to Georgia to start studying there as a chiropractor.

I agreed and we had a magical couple of nights in Miami. On one of these he produced a box with a beautiful diamond and Tanzanite white gold ring that he'd had made for me.

'I've met the woman of my dreams,' he said as he gave it to me.

I felt so special. At the same time I had a knot in my stomach. But I chose to ignore it.

We travelled to Vegas, went to a few casinos, then put his belongings in a truck and took a road trip across the States to

Atlanta. That was the first time that I really started to spiritually 'feel' America. Driving through Texas we saw a tornado on the horizon. I'll never forget that. And as we approached Atlanta, I had a grim sense of whirlwinds swirling and men fighting. Spiritually I could sense there was anger and danger.

Soon my days and nights in Georgia came to an end and it was time to return to the ship.

When I told Mr Jazzman that I was going back to finish my contract he was really unhappy.

'Why don't you stay and help me settle in? I could really do with you here while I start my course,' he pleaded.

'I can't,' I replied. 'I'm on a contract and I can't let them down.'

To be honest I was also thinking that I really wanted to finish the cruise. The last leg – a transatlantic crossing to Portsmouth – was going to give me a great opportunity to see my family again in England. That was too good to miss.

But none of my reasoning helped.

'You're abandoning me,' he said. 'I think you're going because you want to break up.'

In actual fact, nothing was further from my mind.

In the end, we had a tense farewell, and I returned to the ship and missed him dreadfully. I wrote letters constantly and sent him photos, but all he was really concerned about was the other 'hot guys' in the crew. He was terrified that I was going to meet someone else. But I was in love with him. Being faithful to him for me was a no-brainer.

Mr Jazzman, however, didn't see it quite like this, and I noticed when I phoned him he was becoming more and more distant as the weeks rolled by, even though he said he wanted me to come and live with him in Atlanta.

I saw out my contract on the cruise ship and, after docking in Portsmouth, visited my family in England. It was the day after Princess Diana had died.

I spoke to my sister and told her that I had met a man who ticked all the right boxes. She told me not to fly back to the States and re-join him in Atlanta.

But that's what I did.

On the way, I decided my plan was to live with him and find a job at a local spa to replenish my depleted funds while he became a fully qualified chiropractor. But when we had our reunion at the airport, I could tell something was wrong. He was cold and remote, and he seemed strangely detached when we hugged.

And then the criticisms started.

'What have you done to your nose?'

I had had a tiny diamond stud put in especially for him, because I'd heard him say he liked it when he saw another girl wearing one. I thought he'd find it sexy.

'You've gained weight,' he added.

Well, I had, as it happened, and the reason for that was because he didn't want to take responsibility for birth control so I had to go on the pill. Not only did it make me put on weight, it also made me feel very sick. I even had fainting fits because of it.

The sniping didn't stop there.

'Why are you wearing those awful denim dungarees?'

'Why have you come over with such little money?'

I felt crushed.

I moved in with him and started looking for jobs so I wouldn't have to be criticized for not paying my way.

As I was doing that, I found myself alone one day in our apartment. I was surfing the channels when I discovered a preacher called Creflo Dollar on one of the God channels. He was a brilliant communicator and my attention was arrested. His church was also nearby in Atlanta. I can't remember exactly what he said, but something really got to me and I knew what I was hearing was important. So I started to try to read the Bible that the American footballer and his wife had sent me.

When Mr Jazzman came home from class I would talk to him about it, but he wasn't interested. We were taking diverging paths. It was just like my marriage had been. History seemed to be repeating itself.

Finally, things came to a head.

I'd managed to get a job working in a health food store while waiting for an opening in a local spa, but his patience had run out.

'Go back to New York,' he shouted, 'and sort yourself out!'

I was completely floored. I had really let my guard down and fallen for this guy big-time. Now I felt utterly rejected and humiliated.

And I was on my own again.

I didn't have a car. All my belongings were in Westport. But I didn't have the money to get there.

Once again I was going to need the help of the unknown God of the universe.

20

Going South

It was as if I was in a black hole – a deep pit of despair in which thoughts of suicide were never far away. Those familiar with this cave of sadness know it to be the darkest and bleakest of places – a place where there seems to be no end to the encroaching grip of powerlessness and hopelessness. Some people never emerge from it alive.

I had managed to find my way back to Connecticut thanks to a loan from my brother. I had found a decent car and loaded up my belongings and driven north to stay with my ever-patient friend in her home in Westport. I had also managed to find a job in a well-respected spa in Ridgefield.

On the outside, everything looked fine. But inside, my heart was breaking.

The heartache from Mr Jazzman was indescribable. I felt as if someone had pulled the plug out and I had nothing left to give.

It all came out one day after I'd finished giving a massage to a lovely client. My practice was never to reveal anything about my private life. The priority was to let clients share about what was on their hearts – if they wanted to speak at all. We had had many deep conversations in which she'd talked about very similar struggles to mine. I had spoken briefly about my life during these times.

'What's happening with Mr Jazzman?' she asked.

At that moment the dam burst and I began to cry.

'My world's fallen apart,' I sobbed. 'I'm barely keeping it together.' And then I added, 'it feels as if God has left me.'

That final remark shocked me, even as I said it.

It was the first time I had ever acknowledged to someone else the existence of the unknown God of the universe – of someone or something watching over me. I had spoken to others about the Universal Energy and so forth. But I had never gone this far and acknowledged that God – whoever or whatever that was – was present in my life.

Only he wasn't present.

He felt far away.

I was overwhelmed by the absence of God.

As harrowing as this was, at least it gave me some co-ordinates concerning where and what to look for in my life. If I felt gutted that God was absent, then that meant the priority was to search for him, to discover at long last who this really was.

As I sat slumped on the floor, leaning against the massage table (my client still lying there), I at least understood what I was longing for.

I needed to know the unknown God.

Over the next few weeks and months I continued to live with my friend in Westport and work at the spa in Ridgefield, all the while asking the unknown God where he was, asking him where I should be.

But there was no answer.

It was as if I was at the bottom of a well, huddled up in my pitch-black surroundings, hiding from the world. It took every ounce of energy I had to keep putting one foot in front of the other, doing my job to the best of my ability, giving my all to my clients.

I took comfort from the music of Bob Marley – constantly amazed by how it spoke about God so much – taking regular exercise and writing my journal.

The answer to my prayers for direction eventually came after my sister's wedding in England, an event which made me genuinely happy for her, but also accentuated the Mr Jazzman-shaped gap at my side. After the wedding I had flown back to the States and joined my friend again at her house in Westport. She was also a massage therapist and had been asked to provide massages for a client's twenty-first birthday. The client asked for two massage therapists so my friend took me.

It turned out that the client was only in Connecticut temporarily. Her boyfriend had his main home on Palm Beach Island in Florida. At the end of her party, she approached me.

'That was one of the best massages I've ever had,' she said.

'Thank you,' I replied.

'Is there any way you could come down to Palm Beach to our home there?'

'I'm very flattered,' I replied, 'but I have a full-time job here in Connecticut.'

'Is there no way?'

'I'll consider it. I don't yet know where I'm meant to be next.'

Not long after that I was given a further prompt. An old friend phoned me – one I'd hung out with when I was married – to tell me she was splitting from her husband and moving to Jupiter, in Palm Beach County, Florida.

This felt as if God was steering me, not least because I'd already been feeling a pull to relocate in the south. I therefore flew down for a visit and sensed that this was where I was meant to be, so I worked out my notice at the spa. I then packed all my belongings into a rented truck with a flatbed carrying my car behind it.

When I said my goodbyes it was a bittersweet moment. I felt as if I was saying farewell to the north, but at the same time I was excited that I was being guided by God into a new place and a new adventure.

As I drove all the way from Connecticut to Florida there was plenty of time to think and to talk to the unknown God. I resisted the urge to switch on the radio and fill the cab with the sound of music. I needed time to reflect and to pray. I had a deep sense that something significant was about to happen, but I questioned what God was saying to me, was he really calling me to go to church. The only thing I knew was that it was time to start trying to visit church more regularly than on a one-off basis. In itself, that was not surprising for a spiritual seeker like me. But it was a new focus compared to everything before.

This didn't mean that I stopped trying to find answers down other spiritual avenues. In fact, I stopped in Georgia en route to Palm Beach County to visit a dear friend I'd met at a sweat lodge retreat. On the way there I started to get the strangest craving for chicken. Given that I was a vegetarian at the time this was totally bizarre. When I arrived at my friend's house, we hugged.

'It's dinner soon,' she said.

'Oh good, what are you cooking?'

'Well, it's a bit odd because I know you're a vegetarian, but I had this really strong sense that I should cook you chicken, so I am!'

As if that wasn't random enough, during dinner she provided another surprise.

'I believe it's time for me to initiate you as a Reiki master,' she said.

'Are you a Reiki master now?' I asked.

'I am,' she replied, 'and that means I can initiate others as Reiki masters too, if they're ready.'

It was all a little surreal to say the least. I managed to eat a little chicken and was asked to stay several more nights, seeing as I was about to be initiated.

That night I didn't sleep well. I tossed and turned repeatedly, disturbed by the sense of an unfamiliar and also unwelcome presence in my room. I put it down to exhaustion.

Over the next few days I was duly initiated as a Reiki master. I remember there were what felt like warning bells going off inside me, but I really didn't understand what that was so I took no real notice. I chose instead to believe that this was the significant event that I had been anticipating in my new move down south. After all, my friend and I had come to believe during a meditation in the sweat lodge retreat that we were sisters in a past life. We had become firm friends with a close spiritual bond. When she initiated me as a Reiki master, I decided that this was just an extension and an expression of the mystical connection between us.

I left Atlanta and drove the rest of the way to my friend's house in Jupiter, Palm Beach. When I arrived I was really excited. There were small but lovely condos everywhere, with neatly manicured gardens, palm trees, and a glorious beach within walking distance.

It was fantastic to see my old friend. We had always got on really well. In fact, my ex-husband always used to refer to us as 'Fire and Gasoline'. If we'd been like that when married, think what we were like now that we were both single! Fun times lay ahead.

That first night, however, I was woken up by my heart beating extremely fast. I felt sick. I then felt pain in my chest which extended up into my throat. I thought I was having a heart attack.

I sat up and took my pulse, then went downstairs to my friend's bedroom and told her about my symptoms. She put it down to exhaustion from all the driving, gave me a glass of cold water and some ibuprofen, and suggested I lie down and try to cool off.

I went back upstairs, and as I lay down again I felt a strange spiritual presence in the room. I couldn't tell you if it was good or bad, but that I was aware I was not alone.

The next thing I remember was my friend calling to me in the morning, saying she would leave keys on the kitchen counter for me as she was off to work.

Over the next few weeks she showed me round the area and we had a lot of fun. However, my funds were now running really low and I needed to find a job. I had no way of knowing yet if my massage client I had met in Connecticut would become my ongoing client, so I had to find something in-between. I had to act fast, so once again I prayed to the unknown God.

Shortly after, I was invited to go to a local arts and crafts fair at one of the nearby parks. While walking around I stopped to look at some wind chimes while my friend carried on ahead of me. Suddenly I heard her calling me. She was standing by what looked like a medical tent. I rushed over to her, wondering what on earth was happening, and found myself face to face with a tall, grey-haired, blue-eyed man.

This gentleman was into something called 'sound healing'. He had developed a machine that sent sound through the body. It used music and vibration to heal ailments. He had been explaining the machine to my friend when she had mentioned I was a massage therapist and needed a job. He said they were looking for someone.

I was so happy. It felt like there was a real chance I would be hired by this group. They were attached to the local hospital. The group were very committed to alternative medicine using New Age practices, yoga, meditation, acupuncture, colour therapy, sound therapy and herbal remedies. I loved all these, so it felt like the perfect fit.

I was asked to submit a résumé and later to go for an interview. This went very well, and eventually I was offered the job after a few nail-biting days of waiting.

I was so relieved; I didn't want to rely on my friend for money. I had a job I loved and I could pay all my bills and expenses.

It was now time to build up my client base, so I contacted the woman whose boyfriend had a house in Palm Beach and whose birthday party I had gone to up north. She said they were still in Connecticut. They were 'snow birds' – people who came to live in the south during the snowy months in the north. She said they would be back soon and that I could see them then.

It seemed that going south was just what the unknown God had wanted for me.

It was time to make a fresh start.

Part III
Coming Home

The ache for home lives in all of us – the safe place where
we can go as we are and not be questioned.
Maya Angelou, *All God's Children Need Traveling Shoes*
(New York: Vintage, 1991)

21

Come to My House

Doesn't it strike you as strange that church is so often the last place people try to find spiritual fulfilment? Is that because we have some inbuilt resistance or even hatred towards the concept of church? Or is it because deep down there is some force at work in our lives that's hell-bent against us finding the light?

Speaking for myself, I had tried pretty much everything, at least as far as mystical practices were concerned. I had engaged in past-life regression, shaman walks, ashram retreats, guided meditations, Reiki healing, New Age crystals, psychic consultations. You name it, I'd done it. I'd even had a brief interest in witchcraft.

Why, then, had I avoided one of the most obvious sources of spiritual guidance, namely the church?

That question seemed even more important to me now that I had arrived in Florida and started a new life. On the way down, single-handedly driving a rental truck with all my belongings, I had sensed God inviting me to his house. In fact, during all those lonely hours of travelling that was the one thing I thought I had heard him say.

It was time to try church.

But where was I to start?

The answer came when I was introduced to an English lady whom I will call Blondie. No prizes for guessing why. She was a very pretty, slim, blonde and bubbly lady who wanted to try going to church. As it transpired, the main reason for this was because she was looking for a wealthy husband. But I didn't care about that.

Blondie and I set off on our church hunt – or 'husband hunt', in her case. We tried a few churches but didn't sense any kind of presence or any spiritual connection. Until, that is, we arrived one Sunday morning at Christ Fellowship, a huge congregation in West Palm Beach. As soon as we walked in, we both felt it – this reassuring presence, this sense of this was where we were meant to be, this sense of arriving.

For me, it was as if I had finally come home.

As the weeks went by, I began to learn more and more about the Bible, and consequently more and more about light and darkness. I was still dabbling in other mystical practices but as I heard the Bible being taught I became more and more uneasy about some of the things I had been into spiritually. But as much as that sense of internal conflict grew, I still couldn't give up my yoga, tarot cards, crystals, runes, meditation, numerology, feng shui and so on. I wanted to know what the future held.

At the same time I began to notice that psychics rarely seemed to say anything about the future. Their insights were mostly historic – about the past. I was disillusioned that they could never say anything definitive about what lay ahead.

I also began to feel more and more uncomfortable in the New Age store I'd been frequenting. There was a feeling of unease in my spirit. It didn't sit right.

For the next few weeks I looked for answers in both the church and in New Age practices. At the same time, my relationship with my housemate in Jupiter broke down when she started having an affair with a married man. I'd seen the damage done to my parents' marriage by my father's affair. I had made an inner vow that I would never knowingly be responsible for the breakdown of someone else's relationship.

As our paths began to diverge, I felt very low and thoughts of suicide began to arise once again. I couldn't really understand why. Perhaps it was because I hadn't achieved what I thought I would by this age. I wasn't married. I hadn't found true love. I didn't own my own home. I was still living under someone else's roof. And now my housemate and I seemed to be drifting away from each other and I was no longer free to share my heart with her.

A few nights later these feelings assailed me with a vengeance. I lay on my bed with my Bible asking God what was wrong with me. A grim heaviness came over me, settling like a black shroud. I found every tablet in the house – mostly sleeping tablets – and prepared myself to take them. This seemed like the best way to go; just like falling into a permanent and peaceful sleep, never to wake up again to this continuous nightmare.

I placed the tablets across the bed. Just as I was about to take them, I asked God one more time, 'What's happening to me?' As I did, an extreme tiredness suddenly swept over me.

I hadn't taken any of the tablets so it wasn't anything chemical. As the tiredness began to take effect, I looked out of the bedroom window into the moonlit night. As I did, my eyes began to fix on the moon. There was something shining right in the centre of it.

As I stared at it, I rubbed my eyes.

Is that . . . is that a cross?

In the centre of the moon was a cross. It was the same colour as the moon only shining more brightly. It seemed to be coming out of the centre towards me.

With that my eyes closed and I yielded to the tiredness. I fell into a deep sleep.

The next morning I woke up on top of the bedcovers with some of the tablets stuck to my face.

I brushed them off, got up, and went to work in a daze.

What happened to me last night?

I couldn't answer the question; all I knew was that someone really was watching over me, stopping me from taking the pills, and keeping me alive. Maybe there was a reason why I was on this earth, a purpose worth fighting for, some cause for hope, however frail.

From that day on I worked even harder at the medical centre, trying to build up funds to get my own place. In the process I began to gain a bit of a following at work.

One day a new client came in. I felt an immediate affinity with her and sensed we were going to become firm friends. There was just something about her, but I didn't know what that was – yet. Then it transpired in a conversation that she went to the same church as me, Christ Fellowship! Since it was such a massive congregation it was easy to miss someone.

But from that time on we became good friends. She encouraged me to keep pursuing God through Christianity. Often she would give me a quote from the Bible to inspire me, and this gave me a deep hunger to read the Bible more and find out where these passages came from.

Then a new receptionist joined our practice. She was a committed Christian too. We would often talk to one another about God.

It seemed that I was having more and more meetings with Christians outside of church.

I was pursuing God.

Maybe he was pursuing me too.

While this was all happening, I had this growing sense of trust in God that he would provide for me in all my needs. If I believed in him and trusted him, I knew that I would eventually have the funds to have my own place and restart my own business. Even so, I was not bold enough yet to take the leap of faith required to leave my current job and reactivate Heartfelt Touch. I had a few private clients at this stage, but not enough to overcome my trepidation and take the risk.

But God had other ideas.

A new client started coming for treatment. He had been in some terrible accidents. My heart went out to him so I gave him the very best treatment I could. He said it was the best massage he'd ever had. From that moment on he started coming regularly to me.

When he found out I was saving for my own place to live he started tipping me. After a few sessions when he'd not done that, he left $100 on the counter to make up the shortfall. I hadn't seen it because I'd moved into another room to work on a client who required a special bed.

When I came out of my session, I was summoned to my manager's office.

'What's the meaning of this?' she said, indicating the $100 bill.

'What do you mean?' I replied.

'I've been wondering what the secret was behind your growing client list. It seems I've found it,' she retorted.

Then the penny dropped.

One of the other therapists in the office had begun to resent the increasing numbers of people wanting me to give them treatment, and had levelled an accusation that I was offering them what is known in the trade as 'a happy ending' – in other words a sexual favour.

'You think that money is for sex?' I gasped.

'Yes,' she replied.

She couldn't have been further from the truth. In fact, I used to pray a prayer before every massage session, 'Lord, allow me to be a channel of your healing love and light.' This was the secret behind my growing list of clients.

As I looked at my manager, I was devastated. This wasn't the first time that such an accusation had been made against me. It's a charge often made against massage therapists. We are easy targets for such offensive suggestions.

I felt sick. My integrity had been called into question. A colleague had brought a false charge against me. I felt utterly betrayed.

'I can't work under these conditions,' I said to the woman. 'I'm handing in my notice.'

With that, the decision I'd been postponing was now forced upon me. I now found myself having to take the leap of faith to restart my business, whether I liked it or not! It seemed God had pushed me out of the nest and it was now up to me whether or not I spread my wings to fly.

Fortunately for me I now had an excellent reputation so it wasn't long before word-of-mouth recommendations led to a healthy list of clients. I was amazed how people were coming to me even without me advertising. I really could trust God to meet my needs.

As the days went by I began to love my job more and more. I went into some beautiful homes and met some wonderful people. I was even given an open door into the local baseball stadium and acquired some famous professional sportsmen as clients. It was a really positive season, feeling confident in my abilities and being paid for doing something I adored. Plus I found my own apartment just five minutes from the beach. And I managed to buy a nearly new SUV in which to lug all my equipment around.

More important than all of this was my enjoyment of Christ Fellowship.

I had found a church.

I had found my spiritual home.

Furthermore, God was healing me from the inside out.

Everything was beginning to fall into place.

Now all I needed was to find true love.

22

Mr Charming

Although it was great to have my own place, I found my sense of isolation intensified after moving into my new apartment. My family was thousands of miles away, and making new friends was proving to be a slow process. I had to be careful with money having just set up my new home, so it wasn't easy to go out and socialize. Being self-employed was also sometimes unpredictable. If a client was on holiday or ill, then I wouldn't get paid. The summer months were the worst when my 'snow birds' were away up north. The income would dry up but my bills would be the same.

What I was deep down longing for was love, but I was sick of game players and mamma's boys. I wanted an exciting boyfriend . . .

Just as I was drawing closer to God and trusting him more, a new client started coming to Heartfelt Touch. He was a nice guy and we clicked straight away. We had a lot of things in common. When he asked me out, I stood true to my principles to begin with. 'I don't date clients,' I would reply.

But over time my commitment to my rules waned. He was cheeky and made me laugh. He even dumped me as his therapist just so he could ask me out. Like me, he was into healthy foods and working out. He had been the CEO of a golf club hotel and spa, so he had accomplished something in life, even if he didn't have a job at the time I met him. Best of all, he went to the same church as me.

In the end I said yes to the offer of a date and he proceeded to sweep me off my feet. Every time he saw me he gave me the most beautiful flowers. He took me to some top restaurants, and when it was my birthday he took me on a surprise trip to the Bahamas, and a day out to a private island.

It was a whirlwind romance and once I gave way to the physical side of our relationship I was completely hooked. I figured that since he was a Christian, had been raised as a Christian, and was knowledgeable about spiritual things, he would know how we were meant to conduct ourselves. I looked up to him and deferred to him in our decision-making. I didn't think anything of it when he started to tell me how to wear my hair, what clothes to dress in, who to hang out with. My mum had always told me, 'You need a good man to take care of you.' Mr Charming was a strong man. He seemed to know what was right, and was just the kind of man I needed.

When Christmas came round he showered me with presents. Indeed, in all my life I'd never seen so many presents for me underneath a Christmas tree. He spoiled me to bits. But it came with a price tag. Another side of his personality began to emerge. He started to get mad at me for not making enough fuss over the gifts he'd bought for me. And then he got angry that I hadn't spent as much on him – something which I couldn't have done anyway, given the bills I had to pay. Plus I'd sent a Christmas gift to my family back home and I was giving financially to the church. I had no room to manoeuvre when it came to extravagant gift-giving.

I felt sad instead of joyful as Christmas Day wore on. I blamed his mood swings on myself. I tried to make the best of it, but I broke down in tears when I went to the bathroom. We were supposed to be celebrating our first Christmas together. I felt utterly crushed. I came out of the bathroom and made light of it for the rest of the day, but deep down I was confused. How could he be Prince Charming one minute and a raging bull the next?

And how could he be like this and a Christian?

I gave him the benefit of the doubt and put everything down to the stress he was under while trying to find a new job. I made it my aim to become the woman I thought he wanted me to be. Any faults or failings I attributed to my own weaknesses. After all, I had had a failed marriage and a number of broken relationships. I was the common denominator in all of these. Maybe I was the problem.

We carried on into the New Year and then Mr Charming started to give some worrying hints that he had connections with the Mafia. I asked some questions designed to tease more information out of him. He lit up as he started to tell me stories. He told me that he had been trained to kill a person in such a way that no trace could be found. He also intimated that he had done this himself. I didn't believe him. I thought he was just being insecure.

We took a trip to England together to meet my family. It was the first time I'd ever taken a man to meet them. It was not a happy experience. When we arrived at the town where my mum lived I was so excited I wanted to see her straight away.

'We'll go tomorrow,' he said.

'Let's go today,' I replied.

'Tomorrow,' he repeated.

'You've got to be crazy,' I blurted out. 'I'm seeing her right now.'

He was furious. It was awful, but as usual I rationalized it, this time by telling myself that couples sometimes fight with each other even in the best relationships.

I went to visit my mum alone. She and my family thought it strange that Mr Charming wasn't there too.

'He's really tired,' I explained. 'He'll meet you tomorrow.'

When they eventually did meet him, they didn't like him and simply couldn't understand what I saw in him.

When we returned to Florida, Mr Charming proposed to me and took me to see a ring in a jewellery shop in the Bahamas. I accepted but I also asked for the ring to be altered after I found out that it was one he had given to a former girlfriend.

Now that he had told me he wanted to marry me, Mr Charming decided to move in with me. Despite all the red flags, I agreed. When he did, he shared that he had been married before and that his ex-wife had been a 'psycho' who'd made all kinds of accusations against him. Even at the time I questioned whether his wife's side of the story might be very different, and wondered what she was truly like.

I discovered the answer a few weeks later.

I'd applied to go on a women's day at church. When I arrived I went to sign in and noticed a familiar name. *I know that name*, I thought. It was his ex-wife's. I felt my stomach lurch.

As I took a seat I glanced around, wondering which lady she was. I didn't have to wait long. I overheard the woman in front of me talking to her neighbour. As they introduced themselves I discovered that I was right behind her.

My heart started racing. I really wanted to talk to her but I figured to do that at the beginning of the class probably wasn't the smartest move, so I waited till it was over and found a moment to approach her.

I really didn't know what I was going to say, but I felt that God had put her in my path. As she was walking alone outside, I said, 'Hi!' and quickly introduced myself.

I had hoped she could shed some light on what I was going through. I knew something wasn't right, but I felt powerless to sort it out and I needed a life raft. But she rebuffed me. In fact, she got quite hostile and wanted to know why I thought I had the right to even approach her and mention his name. I was shocked. I had not wanted to hurt her in any way. I was just trying to reach out, woman to woman, and had not expected her to be so harsh.

What made it worse was the fact that we were in a church setting. I was new to hearing wonderful things about God and yet here was a 'sister in Christ' being aggressive when I was crying out for help.

She said that she was still in therapy for what he had done to her and she didn't appreciate me flaunting myself in front of her.

That's all she had to say.

I walked to my car, shaking. I had come away with more questions than answers. Should I tell Mr Charming that I had met his ex? Was I now in an abusive relationship, destined to a rollercoaster of emotional highs and lows? How bad did it have to get before I said, 'I'm out of here'? And who would believe me anyway? When we were out in company, everyone thought he was charming. Behind closed doors, however, he was becoming a completely different person.

After months of feeling that the sun was shining on my life, the storm clouds were now well and truly gathering again. In my turmoil I sought answers outside the church, this time through astrology. I didn't realize as a seeker that the Bible discourages us from consulting the stars and urges us instead to trust the God who created the stars. There was a time in my life when I wouldn't make a single decision without consulting my astrologer. I never realized how bound I was by this practice, and how astrology didn't bring me either freedom or a true insight into my future.

This time, however, it was Mr Charming who suggested we should go. I assumed, because he had been a Christian a long time that astrology was therefore OK. We went two or three times to the astrologer, and then he told the woman reading our charts that I needed to go on my own from now on and that she needed 'to sort me out'. She readily agreed. She seemed quite smitten with him.

Having my chart done with that lady never helped. If anything, it made the turmoil inside worse. I really felt that it labelled me and basically said, 'This is your chart, you're stuck with it; this is who you are and this is going to happen to you.' I felt trapped and controlled by it.

Then, Mr Charming and I took a trip to Atlanta to stay with a close friend of his who was a nutritionist and a psychic. Mr Charming believed I was deficient in something, so she carried out some blood tests and prescribed oestrogen. She seemed to think she had all the answers, that she was some kind of super-spiritual goddess. I remember thinking that maybe she was wrong. But I took the hormone anyway. She was just as convincing as my boyfriend. It ended up making me ill, and when I went to my gynaecologist back in Palm Beach she said I needed to come off it immediately. To correct the imbalance she then had to prescribe progesterone. That sent my moods haywire.

Things began to come to a head at church of all places.

One Sunday morning we went to the service together. At that time we often went twice a week. On this particular day, Mr Charming proceeded to stare at an attractive woman in the congregation. He did this throughout the service, even smiling at her at one point.

'Do you know that lady?' I asked him.

'Don't be stupid. Of course I don't! You're just being stupid and jealous.'

I piped down and shut down. I simply couldn't believe this was happening in church.

When we walked out of the church and made our way to the car, he snapped at me, 'Why aren't you holding my hand?'

It was so sudden that I didn't know what to say. All I knew was that it didn't feel safe to get in the car with him.

'I'll make my own way home,' I said.

I began to march out of the parking lot, but he drew alongside me in the car and started screaming in front of all the other churchgoers who were leaving, 'Get back in the car. Get back in the car right now!'

I was mortified.

Then, just as suddenly, it was as though a switch was tripped and his mood completely changed. He started to cry.

'I'm really sorry,' he sobbed. 'It's my job situation. I'm under so much stress not having one. It's killing me.' He paused to wipe his eyes. 'I'm an idiot, I really am. I don't deserve you. You're too good for me. Just be patient with me, please.'

After about ten minutes of this I eventually gave in and climbed into the car.

When we returned to my apartment, we sat on the sofa at a ninety degree angle to each other. I tried to broach the subject of what had just happened.

'If you really want to sort things out, then there's no time like the present,' I said.

That was like casting a lit match into a drum full of petroleum. He exploded with rage, hurling abuse at me. His eyes were wild. In fact, if I have ever seen the devil's eyes, it was at that moment. I looked away.

'Why are you looking away from me?' he shouted.

'I don't want to say,' I replied.

I felt very vulnerable, and wanted him out of my apartment.

I walked out of the living room into the kitchen so that at least I had the counter between him and me.

He strode to the counter shouting insults and abuse as he drew closer.

Suddenly I felt this surge of energy and authority rising up from deep within me.

I slammed my hand down on the work surface and shouted, 'How dare you speak to a daughter of the Most High God like that? You have no place here. Get out, in Jesus' name!'

His face changed immediately.

He was speechless.

His shoulders slumped forward and then he walked out, not saying a word.

I was in shock.

What on earth just happened? I thought.

23

Devil's Eyes

In the midst of the turmoil with Mr Charming, my oasis of calm and comfort were the services at Christ Fellowship. I loved singing worship songs in the Sunday services and often found myself automatically raising my hands in worship. Once when I did that Mr Charming grabbed my hands and forcefully placed them back at my side, snarling that no one else did it. I remembered being embarrassed and humiliated so I prayed a quiet prayer while everyone else was worshipping God. 'Lord, what can I do for you?'

I sensed him reply, 'Sing to me,' followed by, 'Join the choir.'

So I did.

I was shaking on the day of the auditions. I nearly didn't go at all. I felt like a fraud when I got there. I was surrounded by all these great musicians and singers. I was out of my depth, but I longed to be a part of such a great choir. I loved music and I knew that music had the power to touch a person's soul, whatever language they spoke. I also knew it had the power to heal. I was desperate to be involved.

I was so touched and humbled when they accepted me, saying that I had a good range as a singer, but that they were going to use me as an alto for the time being.

So now I was part of the choir!

From then on, every time I sang I felt this powerful presence. Later I discovered that this was what they called the 'Holy Spirit'. But at the time, all I knew was that when we sang, the presence was so strong on occasions that it took all my strength not to fall down.

Every time I reached up in praise, it seemed as if the unknown God of the universe reached down to me. This gave me reassuring moments of serenity during the terrible turbulence raging in my life.

From the time of my confrontation with Mr Charming, I really began to question our relationship. I learnt in church that it was not God's plan for us to have sex outside of marriage. It confused me that Mr Charming said that it was OK. It confused me even more when he wanted to introduce pornography into our life together, 'to spice things up'.

'Why do we need that?' I asked. 'It makes me feel dirty and unloved, that I'm not good enough.'

'I just need a little extra something,' he replied.

'But I thought the Bible forbade sex outside marriage.'

'You're just being literal in your interpretation,' he replied. 'That's not what the Bible really teaches.'

But I knew enough already from previous encounters that sex was more than a purely physical act – that in intercourse two people were joined spiritually. Even if I was not able to understand everything the Bible taught, I at least understood that. My problem was not that I didn't believe sex outside marriage was wrong. It was that I couldn't live long without it. I needed it to feel affirmed, wanted, loved.

Things came to a head one day when I went round to Mr Charming's motel room. By now he had moved into his own place. I asked him to leave because I no longer felt right about living together.

I was sitting at his computer. He had given me permission to use it. While I waited for something to download, I caught site of a printout of a busty woman in the accordion file that had fallen open under his desk.

My heart started racing. I knew this wasn't going to be good news.

He was on the bed behind me, reading something for an upcoming job interview, so I knew he wasn't watching me.

I seized my opportunity and pulled the piece of paper out of the file. It was a printout of email exchanges between him and this woman.

I felt sick; my heart was thumping. I started breathing faster.

What's going on? Why is my fiancé exchanging emails with this woman?

I checked the dates in case it was before he and I had started our relationship. It was recent. In fact, it was right after he had proposed.

I delved into the same file and found a stack of emails with other women. I use the term loosely because a transvestite had also been corresponding with him. It quickly became clear that these were escorts. While I had been out earning money, working hard with my business, he had been busy with these ladies rather than diligently hunting for jobs.

By now I was shaking and my mouth had gone dry. I didn't know what to do, I was scared – scared to move, scared to say anything, scared of his reaction. Despite being taller than him, he did bodybuilding and was in really good shape, so I didn't want him to fly into a rage.

Nonetheless, something inside me forced me off my chair. I knew I had to talk to him. Maybe I was wrong, maybe there was a reasonable explanation? Maybe, maybe, maybe . . . the pattern of making excuses and seeing the best in his motives momentarily stalled me.

The steps I took were only a matter of a few feet, but I felt as if I was in slow motion.

As I reached the side of the bed he looked up. His expression was calm until he saw my face, by now streaked with tears and etched with the question, 'Why?'

'What's wrong?' he asked.

'Who are these women?' I cried. 'What's this all about? What were you doing with them while I was at work? Is that why you kept such a close eye on me all the time? So I wouldn't catch you? What do you get from them that you're not getting from me?'

He tried to offer a feeble explanation.

'It's my friend's fault. He introduced me to this escort scene. I wouldn't have gone near it but I was bored not having a job and stressed not being able to find one.'

'That's no excuse!' I shouted.

He changed tactics. 'Well, if you weren't so boring, perhaps I wouldn't have needed to do it!' he retorted.

I stood there appalled for a second, then threw the printouts in his face.

'You call yourself a Christian? Is this how Christian men treat someone they've asked to marry them? What would our pastor think? I thought you loved me?'

At that he leapt up, grabbed me by the throat and slammed me down on the bed, his fingers squeezing my throat as he shouted abuse.

A memory flashed through my mind of the day he had told me one of his friends in the Mafia had shown him how to strangle someone. At the time I had thought it was just another one of his fantasies and hadn't taken it seriously. Now, as I lay pinned to the bed fighting for my life, I was worried that he'd been telling the truth.

He'd managed to pin me down so that both of my arms were under his legs. I continued to resist and in my mind cried out to Jesus to help me.

I could feel myself blacking out, but somehow got my left leg under him and shoved him away from me.

He fell back onto a little table but came at me again. I thrust him away. His eyes were wild, like devil's eyes.

Now I was making for the front door. As I tried to grab my bag, he made to push me but I dodged him.

'If I can't have you, then no one can!' he roared as he headed for his cabinet where I knew he kept a gun.

I bolted for the door.

I didn't dare look back.

I could hear him trying to unlock the cabinet.

I ran to my car, all the while fumbling in my bag for my keys. I felt as if I was in a movie. I couldn't believe it was happening to me.

I couldn't open the car door quickly enough as he appeared at his front door.

Why wouldn't my hands work?

Just get the keys in the car door, woman!

Finally I managed to get in the car and lock the door.

He was heading my way shouting, but I reversed out of that parking lot like Thelma & Louise. I could see spraying sand in my rear view mirror, my heart pounding violently.

As I sped off, I was choking on my sore throat and tears. My chest and ribs felt bruised where he'd been on top of me.

But I'm tall, I'm strong, how did he overpower me?

'I'm a good person!' I screamed in the car.

'All I want to do is be loved and to love someone and live happily ever after!'

'Why me?'

'What did I do to deserve that?'

'But he's a Christian! God, I don't understand!'

I drove in a haze, scared to go home to my apartment in case he followed me, scared to go to my friend's house because she had warned me against him, she didn't like him – and other stuff we'd fallen out over. Still, I decided to eat humble pie and dialled her number. I pulled over to the side of the road and sobbed as I waited for her to pick up.

She answered, but I couldn't speak at first. All I could do was sob and gasp, but she understood what was going on. She told me to come over to her house right away.

I don't remember driving there. I vaguely recall arriving at her front door. She hugged me and took me inside.

I felt so, so embarrassed, humiliated, confused and ashamed. I couldn't stop shaking. All I kept repeating over and over in my head was, *Is this really happening to me? How did I let this happen? What's wrong with me? What did I do wrong?*

My friend wanted me to go to the police and report what had happened, but I was too ashamed. I said it must have been a one-off and I listed all the excuses I'd made for him. I could see her exasperation mixed with sadness and sympathy. She was livid with him. I sat on her sofa and memories of my parents' fight went through my head. I couldn't help wondering if I was cursed – destined to repeat history.

I told her everything, but hated having to admit that she had been right about him. I could not stop feeling so ashamed. I just wanted to shrivel up and vanish under my duvet.

That night as I lay in her guest bedroom struggling to sleep, I shivered incessantly until finally exhaustion got the better of me.

24

Second Chance

Once I had returned to my own apartment, I started taking long walks along the beach road, trying to clear my head. I was desperately praying that God would show me what to do. I needed guidance so badly.

On one of these walks, a man riding an old-fashioned bicycle passed me and almost got run off the road by a car. I noticed as I approached to help him that there was what looked like a number plate on the back of his bike. It was written in what initially looked like Chinese characters, but the name 'Jesus' seem to spring out of it. It took me by surprise.

'Do you have "Jesus" written on the back of your bike?' I asked.

He looked at me before replying.

'Only those who have him in their hearts see that,' he said.

With that I began to break.

He prayed for me, and I was so grateful that God had heard my cry and sent me such a clear signal that he was watching over me and looking after me.

Another time on the same walk, I was approaching the point where I did my stretches, near the end of my route, where I turned round at the pier in Juno.

I was praising the Lord through my pain when I instinctively raised my hand in worship, completely forgetting where I was. As I did, I noticed an elderly man with a hat sitting on a bench near the beach. He was facing away from me, so he couldn't see me. But as I had raised my hand, he had done exactly the same thing! As soon as he did, I heard a voice inside my head saying, 'Go over and talk to him.' Even though I questioned it at first, I eventually obeyed.

'Hi,' I said.

As he turned round, I saw that his cap had the words 'Jesus loves you' written on the front.

I began to cry.

'I saw you raise your hand when I did,' I said through my tears, 'and I just felt I had to come and say hi.'

'Jesus loves you, sister,' the old man replied, 'and he sent me here today to tell you that. He told me that I would meet someone here who'd need to hear that.'

I sat down next to him.

'Do you mind if I anoint you?' he asked, producing a small bottle. 'God has great plans for your life and he wants to use you.'

I nodded yes and he then proceeded to anoint my forehead and my hands. A deep feeling of peace came over me.

After a while I managed to leave and return to my apartment. But my head was not thinking clearly even if my heart had been comforted. I missed Mr Charming.

That may sound crazy after what he had done, especially to anyone who has never been in an abusive relationship. But it's true. Even though he treated me badly I kept blotting out the negative memories and focusing instead on how generous and romantic he had been. And then there was the great sex. I was missing that too, even though I had also started questioning towards the end whether we should be having sex at all.

After a few months of him trying to contact me, I gave in and agreed to meet up. He invited me to my favourite sushi restaurant and showered me with flowers. It wasn't long before I believed that our fight had been an aberration and that it was time to give him a second chance.

I didn't tell anyone, and especially my best friend. I knew she would think I was crazy. But I was too fragile to take any criticism. And we were already growing apart again. Ever since I had started going to church she'd felt I had been judging her. Nothing could have been further from the truth.

One day Mr Charming contacted me. He told me he had been given a job running a resort on a Caribbean island called Bonaire. He added that he would love it if I would join him for a week.

Thoughts began to swirl around in my head. I remembered that I'd said a prayer for God to remove him from me physically because I felt too weak to resist his charms, and yet, here I was again facing temptation. I realized God had in fact answered my prayer by opening up a job for Mr Charming on an island near Venezuela!

Here we go again. Do I trust him? Does he really mean it when he says he's changed and that he really wants to make things up to me with a lovely trip to this beautiful resort? Maybe getting the job has helped lift his spirits and he'll be back to his old self, the man I first met.

I agreed to go and actually allowed myself to get excited about seeing another island I had not yet seen. Anyone would have been tempted by the offer of a free week in a place renowned for snorkelling, with all flights paid.

I had taken the bait. I would fly down a week after he had settled in.

I arrived all primped and primed, waxed to within an inch of my life, hair and nails done. *Maybe this would be the beginning of a new relationship with him based on respect and love.*

But as soon as I met him the abuse kicked off again. He would compliment me one minute and pick me apart the next. Then he flirted with a woman at dinner, accusing me afterwards of being crazy and imagining it all.

He saved the worst for the end of the week.

Mr Charming took one of the company jeeps and we headed out to explore the island. I saw a great flock of flamingos in a bay feeding on shrimp. It was one of those moments when you just know there has to be a Creator. What else could explain such beauty?

We stopped on a hill overlooking the sea, and found what looked like an unfinished patio area. He suggested we walk over there to catch the view and he surprised me with a bottle of champagne. He told me he loved me and was sorry for the way he had treated me. He said he didn't understand why he did it. He then started to make love to me.

At first I was a bit hesitant but I have to admit the view, the champagne and the thrill of being outside got the better of me so I let things happen.

But after he was finished he said in a low voice, 'You're pathetic. I could kill you out here and no one would find you.'

It was as if shards of ice pierced my soul.

I started to get dressed as quickly as I could while he headed back to the jeep.

I felt as though I was suffocating.

I was screaming in my head, *How could I be so stupid? What was I thinking? Did I hear what I thought I just heard?*

I ran up to the jeep. He was sitting there ready to leave. I didn't know where we were on the island. I didn't know how far away from the resort we were. The landscape we had driven through had been semi-desert. I felt sick.

He looked at me with an expressionless stare and said in a flat tone, 'OK, time to go back.'

I climbed in beside him, trembling, still unsure if I had heard correctly, but too afraid to mention it.

Just when I had convinced myself that I'd misheard him, he said, 'It really is remote in these parts, isn't it? No one would ever find a body out here.'

Now I was really frightened.

I started praying furiously in my head for God to forgive me for being so foolish. I had chosen to ignore the lack of peace I had experienced during quiet times with God prior to leaving for the trip. I had been deaf to the warnings but I asked him to rescue me.

When we arrived back at the resort I made a beeline for the shower where I locked myself in. I turned on the shower to mask the sounds of my sobs. I knew from experience that if Mr Charming heard me he would get angry. I just wanted to get out of there, but I had to wait for my plane the next day. When I came out of the shower I put my poker face on and acted as if nothing had happened.

I barely slept that night, and the next day I got up before him and went out for a walk. I tried to keep myself busy and out of his way before my flight.

Once we were on our way to the airport, I felt such a sense of relief. I kept thinking, 'Nearly there, nearly there.' It was as if I was flying out of hell, not paradise.

We finally arrived at the airport after a silent drive. I leapt out of the jeep and grabbed my bags. He took one from me and walked me to the counter. He had made the arrangements and told me the flight left at a certain time. When we reached the check-in desk the lady said, 'You've missed your flight. The next flight leaves tomorrow.'

For a moment I thought I was not hearing correctly, so I asked her to repeat what she'd said.

When I realized, I started pleading with her to find a way to get me home.

Of course he blamed me.

I said I'd stay at the airport and wait. The lady replied that I couldn't do that because the airport shut down so I was left with no choice. I had to go back to the resort with him.

After a sleepless night I thankfully managed to get on the plane the next day. By the time I arrived home I was like a wet rag.

Over the course of the next week I do not know how I actually functioned. I ended the relationship with him after he was rude to me again over the telephone. I had reached my absolute limit and knew deep inside I deserved better, but it took every ounce of effort to make that decision and stick to it.

This time I knew it was really over.

It had started out in such a promising way, but over the weeks and months it had eroded into this crazy, addictive, unhealthy rollercoaster ride that I knew I couldn't take any more.

I now had that deep empty feeling I had experienced before when everything seemed far away and pointless, like being at the bottom of a black hole.

I tried talking to my best friend but it was clear now that we were too far apart. She said that since I had been going to church I no longer partied like I used to. She clearly didn't know who I was any more, and to be honest that feeling was mutual. Yes, we had had some wild times together. I liked partying. But we had also shared some other great experiences – camping, sightseeing, girly shopping sprees and so on. We'd shared everything about ourselves with one another.

I missed her terribly.

I was now at breaking point.

25

Divine Intervention

I had now reached the lowest place in my life.

My relationship with Mr Charming was over.

My best friend and I had drifted far apart.

Even my apartment was no longer a safe and quiet haven, with my neighbour above entertaining different men so often I thought she was an escort girl. The sounds coming from her apartment went on all night, every night – including the familiar chopping noises of someone preparing to take cocaine.

My business was struggling too – so badly, in fact, that I considered becoming an escort girl myself to supplement my income. I enjoyed sex with men. Why not get paid for it? The old demons I hadn't yet dealt with reared their ugly heads and made me question if I could really trust this God I was learning about in church. What I didn't know at the time was that I was gaining head knowledge about God but hadn't been 'born again' in the Spirit yet.

I dismissed this thought but I was still in dire straits financially, trying to trust God and keep giving to the church.

Then I was introduced to a wealthy new client who wanted massages in his own home. He lived in a beautiful house in a gated community. At the beginning he was very polite, a true gentleman. But as time wore on, he began asking for 'happy endings' to his massages. I resisted, saying that I went to church and it was against my principles to give sexual favours to clients.

But then unexpected bills began to arrive and I just caved in. Instead of trusting God to provide for all my practical needs, I started to agree to the man's requests. As I left his mansion that first time, holding the extra $100 in my hands, I rationalized it by telling myself that at least I had not had sexual intercourse with him. Who was I kidding? Sexual favours were sexual favours, whether I had had full sex or not.

The 'happy endings' continued until I began to feel that the money was tainted and that I had now effectively become guilty of the charge that I had always hated – that massage therapy is a cover for prostitution. So when my client told me there were other friends he wanted to introduce me to who would like the same 'service', I resisted the temptation to say yes, even though my financial situation meant that it was almost unbearably difficult. In the end I stood my ground and said no, resolving instead to trust God.

It was now October 2000. After all the nights without sleep and the days with little work I was at rock bottom. My family were across the ocean, my engagement had come to an end, and my best friend and I were not talking to each other. My clients all seemed to be away and the work that I was able to do had caused me to sacrifice my most cherished principles and to choose compromise over commitment.

I felt alone, afraid and ashamed.

Sitting in my apartment, it seemed to me that I was an abject failure. None of my dreams had come to fruition. It was as if I was an empty shell.

As tears streaked down my face, I picked up the Bible beside me on the sofa.

At first I couldn't read the words because my eyes were so full of tears. But I just knew that if there were any answers right now I'd find them in this book.

So I took it again in my hands and persevered.

I turned a few pages and began to read.

The Bible had opened at John's gospel, with a story about a woman who went to a well to draw water. She was from a place called Samaria. When she arrived, she found Jesus sitting there. He started talking to her, which startled her. Jewish men were not supposed to talk to women they didn't know in public, and certainly not to a despised Samaritan woman. They were the lowest of the low. 'Dirty from the cradle,' was what Jewish men called them.

But Jesus wasn't like other men. He entered into a conversation with her, and before she knew it, he was reading her heart, looking into her soul as if it was an open book.

'You've been married before – five times, in fact,' Jesus said, 'and the man you're living with right now isn't your husband.'

'How on earth did you know that?' she exclaimed. 'You must be a prophet!'

'Let me tell you about your heavenly Father,' Jesus replied, before explaining to her where her need for intimacy could really be satisfied – in loving worship of the Father that he'd come to reveal, the Father she'd been waiting for all her life.

As I read this, it hit me.

I was the woman at the well.

I had been from one relationship to another. I had had more men than I could remember, and the man I'd just split up with was not my husband either. Plus I had always longed for a father's love.

And then there was Jesus.

The way he talked to the woman was kind, not condemning. He seemed to be perfect.

As I thought about him, I remembered the time I'd led a guided meditation group and Jesus had suddenly appeared in the room. I had seen him sitting next to a well and he was beckoning me to come and sit with him.

I thought about the way I had looked to men for what I could only find in Father God.

I began to cry out to the man at the well.

It was like a soul-scream from the very core of my being – a scream of utter despair.

'If you're really real then I need you to come to me right now! I need you to show up for me because if you don't I'm going to end it all. I can't take any more. I feel destroyed.'

All of a sudden it was as if someone had pumped mist into my living room. I choked back the tears and rubbed my eyes. I thought I couldn't see properly because I'd been crying so much. Everything seemed surreal. It was like a dream. But then I heard Jesus say, 'Come before me.'

I found myself on my knees in the middle of my living room with my hands held out. Then I was facedown, too afraid to look up because I sensed Jesus was above me.

I began to feel wave upon wave of love and forgiveness breaking upon me and I heard the words, 'I love you and I have been waiting for you. I have followed you, I have never left you.'

Waves of liquid love were flowing over and into me.

I was pinned to the floor. I couldn't move.

I have no idea how long I was there.

The next thing I remember, I was stumbling to my feet, staggering to my bed. I slept till the next day.

When I woke up I was so excited. I could not stop grinning. It was as if I'd drunk too much coffee. I was buzzing. All thoughts of suicide had gone, and I now had an overwhelming sense that everything would be OK, that I wasn't alone after all.

I could not stop telling my clients about what had happened. I thought I was going to burst.

I didn't realize what I had experienced until later in my journey as a Christian, but as a spiritual person I understood something very special and significant had happened. I had never felt such amazing love and I knew in my soul that I had found what I had been looking for.

In the Bible this experience is called being 'born again' (which Jesus spoke about in John's gospel, chapter 3). When you give up your life of sin and put your trust in Jesus – often at a time when you're desperate and at the end of your tether – the Holy Spirit, the Spirit of God, comes to transform your life from the inside out. This is possible because Jesus came to set us free – free us from sin, and all that would separate us from God. I had said 'yes' to Jesus, who died for me on the cross all those years ago, bearing all *my* sin and shame, and was raised to life again. Through the cross, he had restored my broken relationship with my heavenly Father, and now he had filled me with his Spirit!

This born again experience can be so dramatic that you feel as if you're starting life all over again – that you're living life in all its fullness for the first time. (I must also add here though that sometimes people are born again and it's a quieter experience; they just know something has 'happened' to change them inside. Maybe later they discover the overflowing love of God. This is often called the baptism in, or being filled with, the Holy Spirit of God.)

It was a genuine rebirth. I had opened myself up to the saving love of Jesus, the perfect man.

He was now my Lord and Master.

He was in control of my life, I wasn't.

And he was a man I could trust to cherish and not abuse me, to honour and not to shame me.

He had been watching over my life since the very beginning.

He had been my 'unknown God of the universe'.

All these years I had been looking for him.

But now I had found him.

I had fallen in love with the dark-haired man of my dreams.

26

Clearing the Decks

What had happened to me – my real encounter with Jesus, God the Son – changed everything. But not everything changed immediately. My soul had been deeply infected by many years of wrong choices. The effects of my lifestyle decisions would take time to remove. I had tried so many different types of spirituality and so many different relationships with men that my soul had become deeply disturbed.

Every time I engaged in a spiritual practice I gave the spirit that governs that practice permission to be in my life, to have dominion over me. And I was to learn that these spirits are not benign. They are real, they are dangerous, and they are of the enemy, the devil, not of God.

Whenever I had had sex with a man outside marriage, I had joined with him not just physically but spiritually, so whatever that man was involved in now affected me too.

So when I was born again, although I was forgiven by Jesus for every wrong thing I had ever said or done that the Bible calls 'sin', I wasn't instantly set free from the habits of a lifetime. This would take time.

When it came to relationships, I managed for a while to resist the temptations to go back to my old lifestyle of seeking love and affirmation through sex. Then one day I met a famous Christian sportsman. He was handsome, fit, tall, and – yes, you guessed it – dark-haired. He was also married.

When he asked me for treatment, I was immediately struck by his extraordinary physique and his kind temperament. He told me that his wife had left him.

Things came to a head when I went over to his beautiful house on the edge of a golf course. He had invited me there to massage him and his friend. After a mixture of champagne, pot and the balmy and intoxicating surroundings, my resistance levels were deteriorating. The stars were shining. The crickets were chirping and there was the sound of water flowing somewhere. I'm not proud to say that one thing led to another.

As things seemed to be building towards an inevitable outcome, he suddenly stopped.

'I can't do this,' he said. 'I'm technically still married to my wife. And I'm a Christian. This isn't right.'

He pulled away.

I felt terribly humiliated and desperately frustrated. I couldn't leave quickly enough.

What happened next caused me even more shame.

His friend followed me home to make sure I got back OK.

'Can I come in for a coffee?' he asked.

But it wasn't coffee that he wanted. And I'm afraid the same was true for me. I had been led so far up the mountain that evening and was still at the summit, looking for a way down.

The sportsman's friend was the obvious route.

Still being unhealed and bound in the area of my sexuality, I chose him to climb down. And the next day when I woke up,

I felt dirty – a feeling that was compounded when the sportsman phoned and told me that he was sorry that last night had happened, that it had all been a big mistake, and that he was desperate for me not to spread it around the tabloids.

I felt sick.

His honour was being preserved.

Mine, such as it was, was in tatters.

What an idiot I had been.

Well, that taught me a lesson – it was not enough to keep repeating the patterns of the past when it came to my sexuality. God had better things in store for me. He wanted to deliver me from the lie that I needed sex to feel loved and affirmed, a lie that had entered my life through the wound of sexual abuse. Although it would take time to be fully free from this lie and healed of this wound, I had started on the road towards my freedom.

What, then, about the other source of damage to my soul – my search for answers through the New Age?

If my soul had been damaged through my sexual relationships, it had also been deeply infected by the occult, mystical practices I had engaged in over many years. Although at the time I thought these were harmless outlets for my spiritual quest, I was now realizing that they are far from innocuous in God's eyes, that they are practices which he forbids in Scripture for our protection.

So the word I began to hear was 'STOP'.

In fact, there were two occasions when I almost audibly heard God say STOP.

The first time I was approaching my front door with a large bundle of massage sheets when I heard the word 'STOP' like a shout in my head. Before I took the next step I looked carefully in front of me. There – lying on the path to the front door – was a large, poisonous, cream-coloured snake with an orangey-red stripe on its head. Had I not stopped I would have trodden on it and been bitten. I hadn't seen it because of all the sheets I was carrying.

Another time I was bringing a bundle of dirty sheets home to be washed when I approached my front door. I was going to lean against the front door with my shoulder so as not to put down the sheets when I put the key in the lock. Before I did that I heard that word again in my head.

'STOP!'

I backed off immediately and dropped the sheets to see why I had been warned like this again.

There, on the door, precisely where I was about to place my shoulder was a deadly black widow spider. She had made her home just where I was about to lean.

Once again, I had had to stop for my own protection.

In a sense, both of these incidents were pictures. God was trying to warn me to stop leaning on the dark practices that I'd relied on for so long. They were poisonous, deadly even, to my soul.

I asked God to help me in this and spent time praying, keeping a journal, reading the Bible, listening to sermons at church, watching God TV and generally seeking more of God's wisdom and presence in my life.

During that time of intense pursuit of him, God met me in several critical ways.

One night I was sitting up in bed praying and reading the Bible. I suddenly felt the presence of God all around me.

As I was making notes in my journal I started to write backwards in a language I didn't understand. Then I began to speak out loud in a language I had never learnt.

What was going on? I was freaked out. I threw my Bible down and ran into the living room. I was genuinely afraid because I had absolutely no framework for this experience.

I prayed a prayer, however, felt God's peace, and returned to my bed where I fell asleep.

Later – years later, in fact – I was to learn that this was the Holy Spirit visiting me and that I had received one of his special gifts, the gift of speaking in tongues. From that day on I was able to speak in a private, God-given language of praise. Only God knew what that meant. It was our secret language of love. It was the source of great strength to me spiritually, and still is. (You can find out more about this amazing gift and others in the Bible, in the book of 1 Corinthians, chapters 12 and 14.)

On another occasion I woke up one morning engaged in a conversation with God.

'It's time for you to clear the decks,' I heard him say in my heart.

'What does that mean?' I asked. But I knew.

It meant that it was time to dispose of all my New Age books, tarot cards, crystals, runes, astrology charts, numerology books, shaman pictures and so forth.

As it happened it was a totally free day. There were no appointments in my diary. I took hold of everything I had that was connected to New Age practices and smashed or ripped it up, placing it all in black bin bags. It was important to me that nothing remained intact for someone else to use. I filled at least seven bags.

There was so much stuff, much of which had cost me a lot of money, especially the crystals. I had collected quite a lot of rare ones when I had worked in the New Age crystal store in New York. They were hard to part with because they were large and exquisite. Letting go wasn't easy.

One item that I disposed of dramatically was the crystal bowl that my ex had given me. It was huge and had cost several hundred dollars. I took it out to a remote corner of the parking area. 'For you, Lord,' I said, as I smashed it into little pieces.

That was major.

Once I had got rid of everything I felt amazing. I won't lie, there was a moment when I said, 'What have I done? That was expensive stuff!' But the truth is I was lighter and freer.

I had done what God had asked.

I had cleared the decks.

27

Time to Move

As the summer wore on, I received a vision of the Lord encouraging me to find loads of boxes. I was a little perplexed, but after the third time seeing the same vision I heard him say to me, 'It's time for you to go home. I have a work for you to do.'

Go home? I thought. *This is home. England is where I visit to see my family. But it's not home. This is.*

I remembered a time when I'd been back in England and spoken to my mum's neighbour.

'There's nothing here for me,' I'd told her.

I had made my home in America. I loved the 'can do' positive attitude of the people. I also loved how open they were about their Christian faith. Famous athletes were always unashamed about Jesus in public. There were Bibles on sale even in the supermarkets. To give up my apartment near the beach, my great church, singing in the choir, my business, the friends I'd made – well that would be a *big* step of faith.

But I was now at a crossroads. I knew that if this was really God speaking, then I couldn't renew the lease on my apartment – the apartment I'd worked so hard to afford.

I decided to follow the promptings I'd felt and phone the leasing agent. They didn't answer so I hung up, thinking maybe I had misinterpreted my nudges. But the promptings wouldn't let up so I phoned again and left a message on the agent's answer machine.

Later she rang back. She was surprised because the landlord had told her that morning he was going to sell the apartment and that I'd have to move out. But I had beaten her to it!

God had been very kind. He had warned me in advance that it was time to move and had even encouraged me to find boxes. When the news came, it wasn't therefore a shock. Obedient to God's words, I had already started packing the boxes. But where did he want me to move to?

The thought of moving exhausted me, but I took comfort that Jesus was definitely orchestrating this, so he would guide me to the right location and give me strength. I therefore placed everything in his hands.

'OK, Lord, where am I to live before I leave?'

The answer came to me through friends I had made in the choir at church. Several of the ladies knew about my journey. Although I held back from telling them everything, I had started opening up to other believers, sharing some of my challenges, and asking them to pray for me.

That was a learning curve. I had learnt to go it alone for many years, so it was hard for a while, humbling myself and asking others for help. I'd always presented myself as an upbeat, fun person who didn't have any weaknesses. Now I was learning how to be real. I was moving from independence to interdependence. It was time to overcome my very

British reserve that said, 'You can cope on your own. Stiff upper lip – big girls don't cry – you'll manage.'

It turned out that one of the ladies in the choir wanted to take in a lodger. This offered me a stop-gap solution for a few weeks before a new friend in church said I could move in with her. Her house was twice the size and she was also very respectful of my need for space. So that was a much better fit.

While I was waiting for more guidance concerning my 'call home', everything was put on hold for a season by the awful events of 11 September 2001. Amazingly, right after I had been born again, God gave me a prophetic word that there would be trouble emanating from the Middle East.

On that terrible morning, I woke up, walked into the kitchen and made myself a coffee. I went back to my room to prepare myself for my clients that day when the phone rang. It was a friend who was shouting for me to turn on the TV. A passenger jet had just flown into one of the Twin Towers – a tourist hotspot to which my former husband and I had often taken visitors to New York. I froze. Then I watched stunned as another commercial jet flew like a missile into the second tower, causing a bright orange and red fireball to erupt in the blue, cloudless sky.

There are people in that plane! There are people in that building!

Dark black smoke filled the sky around the tower. Debris fell from the impact spot, including reams of white paper from the offices hit by the jet. I could even see people throwing themselves from the building rather than burn in the flames.

It was horrific. The nation was in shock.

A terrorist attack of massive proportions was taking place on American soil, in the epicentre of New York City, at the headquarters devoted to the country's financial and commercial dealings around the globe.

Everyone's world was shattered. My clients all cancelled. There was a rush on the supermarkets to buy canned food and water. It was utter mayhem.

Even though the attack had happened far away in New York, every state of the USA was on high alert, including my state, Florida. People were phoning from all around the world to check that their loved ones in the USA were OK.

I spoke to my dad, who was now living at my brother's house.

'We think it's time for you to come home,' he said.

It seemed pretty well my whole family agreed. It was my sister, Janet, who was most insistent.

'We can do so much stuff together,' she said, 'like camping in the new caravan, day trips, family dinners . . . you can even come to the polo with my husband. Who knows? We may even be able to introduce you to a nice new guy!'

To be honest, having been away from my family for so long it felt really heart-warming to know I was missed and that everyone wanted me back in England.

And so did God.

This was highlighted for me when I was thinking about how to ship all my furniture and belongings. How was I going to do that?

The answer came from a new friend I'd made in the choir. She was a lovely girl from the Caribbean. One day I was explaining the challenges to her when she interrupted me.

'You'll never believe it.'

'What?' I replied.

'That's my husband's job!'

'What is?'

'He works for a shipping agency. They can move your things.'

What a coincidence – or 'God-incidence', as I was starting to call these kinds of meetings.

I made the decision what to keep, what to ditch and what to sell. I had always invested in quality, so that was tough. Plus there were items that had a close connection to my identity. But I had to be brave and let go. The Lord was calling me to do this. He would give me the grace to make the sacrifices necessary.

My sister began to look for a flat for me back in England while I continued, in spite of my struggles, to make ready. Then a Middle Eastern man with a backpack walked into one of my local restaurants threatening to blow the place up. That provided some extra motivation to relocate.

When the people from the shipping company came to take my belongings from storage, the reality of what I was doing suddenly hit me. I was shaking. I tried to calm down.

'I have a work for you to do'– that's what the Lord said, I kept reminding myself.

I prepared to drive my jeep up to Connecticut, with all my suitcases. The plan was to sell the jeep to friends there and then fly out from the airport where I'd first landed.

That felt kind of symbolic.

As the day for leaving Florida approached, I had a very vivid dream which brought some peace to my apprehensive heart. In the dream I could feel my knees hurting, so I looked down and saw I was kneeling on sandy rock. Then I felt as if my head was wet so I started to wipe away what I thought was either sweat or rain from my brow, because it was getting in my eyes. As I did so I noticed my hand was covered in blood. As I looked down over my body there was blood everywhere. I panicked, but heard a voice say, 'Look up.'

As I did, I saw Jesus on the cross. His blood was dripping on me. He looked at me tenderly and said, 'Don't worry, Deborah. I've got you covered.'

A sense of peace flooded me. Then I woke up.

I lay there in my bed a few minutes trying to take it in. The dream had been so real I could still feel my knees hurting. From that day on I knew I needed to trust the Lord more, and not let worry overwhelm me.

He had me covered.

The dreaded day arrived and I gazed one more time at the sea as I started my long drive north. There were tears in my eyes. I cried and cried as I drove, until at last I felt relief.

When I eventually arrived at my friends in Connecticut, snow was falling. What a contrast!

I handed over the car I had worked so hard for – a nearly new, gold-coloured sports utility vehicle with cream leather interior and all the mod cons. It was the first time I had ever owned such a car. Now it really felt as if my flesh was being crucified, just as the Bible teaches.

Just at the last minute, however, my friends changed their minds.

'We can't afford it after all,' the wife said.

That was a bombshell.

There was only one thing for it. The car would have to be repossessed and that would mean the credit rating which I had also worked so hard to achieve would be ruined. I was gutted. It seemed as if I was being stripped of everything. All I could do was cling to the Lord and a Bible passage that he had given me, from the Old Testament book of Jeremiah, chapter 29, verse 11:

'For I know the plans I have for you,' declares the Lord, 'plans to prosper you and not to harm you, plans to give you hope and a future.'

The next day I was taken to the airport.

I was worried that I would have too much baggage, but I was checked in without a problem.

As I passed through the final gate I turned, pausing to say goodbye to the country where so many memories had been made – and where I had done so much growing up.

Now, aged 36, as I boarded the plane for England, all I could hang onto were the words that I'd heard, 'I have a work for you to do.'

28

Counting the Cost

Landing in England, it was easy to question the move. It had been a huge step of faith to take, and now that the sobering reality of the transition was beginning to hit me, I began to wonder whether it had all really come about primarily because of the pressure of my family's concern for my wellbeing after the 9/11 attacks.

As I walked off the plane I was already missing the cloudless days in Florida, my apartment near the sea, and my successful and fulfilling small massage business.

Had this really been a God-dream, I wondered? Or was it a daydream?

Almost immediately I began to counter my doubts.

Hadn't I sometimes complained about it being hot all the time in Florida?

Wasn't it true that I'd been so sure that God had said he had a work for me to do?

I was going to have to hold out.

Settling into my new life in Somerset was not without its problems. My sister confided that she was going through difficulties in her marriage, and my family members were finding it hard to adjust to me being back in England permanently.

All my rose-tinted pictures of being in the safe and reassuring embrace of my family were now starting to fade. I had been away a long time. Re-entering English culture, not to mention my immediate family, was as tough as reacclimatizing myself to the English weather. There were clearly challenges ahead.

Setting up home sweetened the bitter pill somewhat. My sister was kind to me, helping me to find a flat and then locating a furniture store where I could buy the kind of bed I wanted. After all the time I had spent doing such things on my own in America, it felt good to be supported by someone in my family. But finding a good church was not so easy. I had been part of a really lively and large church in Florida, and had loved singing in the choir. When the people had worshipped God, it was electric. And as I mentioned before outside church contexts, Christians in America were not shy or embarrassed about their faith. They talked about Jesus frequently and easily.

Back in England, the difference couldn't have been more marked. Churches within the locality were not large or lively, and I became distressed by how Christians generally seemed to be so reluctant to speak about personal faith in Christ. It almost seemed as if the name 'Jesus' had become a cultural taboo.

All this came to a head when one day I tried to talk about my faith to my sister and my mother in my sister's kitchen.

'You've gone mad!' they screamed at me. 'You've become obsessed with God and with church. Just a get a job, however small, and be normal!'

The strength of their hostility unnerved me. I hadn't really appreciated how secularized and politically correct Britain had become when I had returned for my short, flying visits in the past. I hadn't been embedded long enough in the culture to see how things had changed.

But now the Holy Spirit was revealing it to me big-time.

Returning to a country where the church had lost its central role in the community, and where secularism had clearly replaced Christianity, was hard for me to take. It clearly grieved the Holy Spirit too.

Shocked by this contrast, it became imperative that I found a vibrant church where people were on fire for God and passionate about their faith. I knew I needed this if I was to stay sane in my transition and be supported during one of the greatest tests of my life.

But at first I was alone, without confident and authentic Christian friends, trying to kick-start my small business in an area where I hadn't worked before and where I wasn't known. Some mornings it was only my faith in God that got me out from underneath my duvet.

Things became even tougher when my sister dropped the bombshell to the family that she was leaving her husband. It was as if a tornado had struck. She had opened up to me about her marital problems. I was now accused by my brother-in-law of aiding and abetting her in her departure.

The chaos that followed was almost unbearable.

My sister disappeared.

No one knew where she was.

But because she had confided in me, it was assumed that I knew her whereabouts. This caused no end of problems; my family members and her friends interrogated me aggressively for information which I didn't have. It became so intense that

I was even scared of going into town in case I bumped into someone who wanted to know where she was now living.

In the end, my sister reappeared and then left, taking her two daughters with her. Part of me was relieved. Even though I probably didn't handle things as well as I should have, I had been caught in an impossible situation and had become a go-between, trapped in the middle between my sister and the family. I was grateful not to be in that position any more, but sad that my dream of happy families had been shattered and the promise of outings with my darlin' sister – camping, dinners and meeting new friends – had not materialized.

And my business was proving hard to get off the ground as well. In fact, I hadn't really appreciated how challenging this was going to be. In America, massage is regarded as a necessity for health and wellbeing. In England, it is looked on as a luxury. In addition I was now in rural England – in farm country, no less – and money was tight. There were massage therapists in the area, but they were reluctant to give advice on advertising or help with contacts. So I was faced with an uphill struggle. It seemed that the door to massage therapy was now closing.

God had said to me that there was 'a work' he wanted me to do. It was hard to accept that this meant something other than massage. But he was also saying, 'I am doing a new thing.' I tried going to the Job Centre to find out what that might be, but I was always treated rudely, and no matter what work I applied for, I was always greeted by the same response: 'You're too qualified to do this job. You'll leave as soon as you find something better.'

Consequently I couldn't find work. Employers wanted young applicants whom they could mould. Apparently, because I was in my thirties, I was beyond moulding.

I was running out of money. Pretty soon I didn't have enough to fill my wreck of a car with petrol – which was appallingly expensive in comparison to US prices. It wasn't long before I didn't have enough money to eat, either.

I told a vicar about this, thinking that he was a caring and discreet person. He took me into a supermarket, wearing his dog collar, and made a big show of paying for my groceries. On the one hand, I was grateful because I was desperate. On the other, I felt humiliated by the very public exposure of my dire financial situation.

Looking back, I know that that was partly my pride. I had been moderately successful in America and had only occasionally been in financial difficulty. Now that seemed far away and long ago. I felt as though I was no one special. No one knew of my achievements. I didn't even have enough money to put milk in my tea. And now a local vicar had paraded my shameful situation in the local supermarket.

In the end I managed to get through this wilderness, mainly thanks to a Christian who was extremely generous. She often used to leave bags full of groceries at my door and became a good friend. She had been heavily involved in the occult, as I had been, but now was a growing Christian. We had a lot in common.

I also started attending a Baptist Church. I met a man there who hosted a once-a-week Christian programme on local radio and who was looking for an assistant. We talked and he asked me to work with him. I was really excited. When

I found out that he lived across the street from me and his studio was in his attic, I was ecstatic.

I developed the idea of doing a weekly segment in which people could share about the life-transforming power of God's love. I wanted to call it *Testimony Times: A Changed Life Will Change Lives*. I have always believed that personal testimony is high in impact. I felt as if I was beginning to catch glimpses of my destiny. I had often dreamed of being involved in Christian broadcasting. This seemed to be the first step towards that dream. But there is a saying, 'New levels bring new devils.' In other words, when we start to make transitions into a new dimension of purpose, the enemy tries to distract, divert or destroy us.

He is a robber.

He doesn't want us to seize our God-given destinies.

So at every transition, he tries his malevolent best to steal this new season from us.

That is exactly what happened to me.

No sooner had this door to Christian media opened than I was afflicted by terrible headaches. Every time I was due to go over to the studio I would suddenly feel this immense heaviness over me. It seemed as if the hordes of hell were against me being involved. In fact, I came to learn that this particular locality was an epicentre for witchcraft and that members of the local covens were furious that the Christian message was being given airtime (and for free) on the local radio.

As I started on my journey towards the 'work' that my heavenly Father had for me, I began to experience severe spiritual attack. This didn't just come in the form of heaviness and headaches. It also came in the form of more temptation.

I had still not completely given up doing massage therapy because I was eager to earn enough money to come off benefits. While I was still trying to find work I was contacted by a very wealthy couple. As soon as I entered their mansion, I sensed the occult atmosphere. They ran retreats for meditation, and engaged in New Age practices.

While I really liked them as a couple, I knew that there were spirits at work trying to tempt me to blend my new Christian beliefs with theirs, or to reject Christianity and revert to my former New Age beliefs and behaviours. I had to stand firm and pray for the protection of the Holy Spirit every time I went.

Problems began to arise, however, when the husband started to make it obvious that he was sexually attracted to me. To make matters even more complicated, he said that he and his group were meant to channel Christ-like messages and energy to the world. As part of that mission, he and the group had decided that I was 'the One'.

'What do you mean?' I asked.

'You're the One who is meant to have my children,' he replied.

Apparently he and the group had been waiting for someone who channelled Jesus just as the man's former, now deceased, wife had done. He and the group had discussed it and agreed that I was the One to do that. He even showed me a property adjoining the mansion, with magnificent gardens and a beautiful view of the sea. He took me on a tour which involved inspecting a hexagonal room with a pulpit, windows nearly all the way round (affording superb views) and a massive amethyst rock in the centre.

I was being offered a place among the wealthy.

I was being offered luxury.

I was being offered intimacy from a tall, handsome stranger.

I was being offered a place in a big family, a spiritual community, an exclusive mystical group.

I was being offered the opportunity of being 'the One' – someone special.

Given all that I have shared about myself, you can probably tell by now how great a temptation that was.

Even with my obvious reservations about bearing his children, this was tough to resist. It was as if the enemy knew my buttons and was pressing them relentlessly.

'You can bring up my children here in this adjoining house,' he said, before adding, 'my wife is OK with this. She cannot have children.'

Although I was in shock, I was also surprised by my reaction.

'I can tell you're attracted to me,' I said, firmly, 'but you need to understand that it is the Christ Light in me to which you're really attracted. You need to return to the true Jesus and start reading your Bible again.'

With that I declined the generous offer to become his concubine, and advised him to be completely faithful to his wife.

I then left the mansion and never went back. I figured that I may have lost the income, but it wasn't worth losing my soul.

As if this wasn't bad enough, on another occasion I went to participate in the fair at a local Methodist church. I set up my massage chair and gave people free back massages using acupressure treatments. I need to add here that when I say 'acupressure', my focus was on specific pressure points in muscles that facilitate relaxation and not on channelling energy or prescribing to any Eastern philosophy. I was also handing out leaflets advertising my business. As I did so, a tall, long-haired man approached me. He was wearing a loud shirt and gold pendants round his neck.

He walked around me three times before he spoke to me.

'My, you're a pretty thing, aren't you? I may have to call on you.'

I thought nothing more of this until a few weeks later when I was in the Citizens Advice Bureau. The same man walked in, sat opposite, and just stared at me. I started praying quietly in tongues and asking God for wisdom. Within seconds I was telling him about God, but as soon as I mentioned the name of Jesus he flew into a rage.

'I abandoned Jesus as a child,' he ranted. 'You are not allowed to mention that name in my presence. Don't you know who I am?'

'No,' I replied.

'I'm the high priest of the local covens,' he shouted. 'And I know who you are,' he added.

It all happened so quickly, but it was obvious that light and darkness had clashed in the Citizens Advice Bureau. The poor clerk at her desk looked totally stunned. Her boss came in and asked the great high priest to leave, and then ushered me politely into the back office. It was interesting, in retrospect, that I was unable to speak the name of Jesus when *I* was heavily into the occult; this man was obviously unable to tolerate that name.

There were other things that happened, too, but these examples show that as I began to catch the first glimpses of my God-given destiny, so the enemy started to intensify his attack.

I was coming to realize that there is a cost when it comes to the high call upon your life.

New levels do indeed bring new devils.

But we have the authority and the power to resist the devil if we are Christians.

And when we do, a little bit more of God's dream for our lives can begin to emerge.

29

A Ladder to Heaven

It has been said that the devil isolates but Jesus integrates. In other words, it is the enemy's strategy to get us on our own rather than living in relationships where we can be vulnerable and accountable.

Jesus, on the other hand, believes in family. In his eyes, trying to manage our lives on our own is sin. Sin in essence is a spirit of independence. It is the prideful attitude that says, 'I don't need God and I don't need other people.'

When we believe the lie of independence, we enter the landscape of isolation.

When we accept the value of interdependence, however, we enter the landscape of healing and hope.

For me, coming back from America was so much tougher than I had anticipated. I had left my church, my community and my friends behind. Separated from the network of people I had built up in Florida, I was now feeling lonely. The sad events which had overtaken my sister had made integration with my own family difficult and isolation easy. I was now in a very dangerous place. So it was no surprise that my old nature reared its ugly head once again, and that I yielded to the temptation to find solace in the arms of another man.

This had been my default setting since a very early age. I had always believed that sexual intimacy was the path to love and affirmation. In reality, of course, it is the road to shame.

Not long after the invitation to bear a rich man's children, I found myself sitting in my flat battling loneliness, putting on a brave face whenever I saw other people. Then a man contacted me. I'd met him a few times before when I had been over from the States visiting my family in England. He had a crush on me, I knew that. When he phoned to ask me out on a date, I initially turned him down. But then doubts began to creep into my mind. Maybe I was judging him too harshly. In the end I agreed to go out with him.

He turned up at my flat and we went out to a local pub for a few drinks. I don't remember whether we had a meal. That whole part of my memory is missing. I'll tell you why.

When we returned to my flat, he asked if he could come in for just one drink. I let him.

'Would you like another glass of wine?' he asked.

I said yes.

He went into the kitchen, poured me a glass, and brought it to where I was sitting. We sat chatting for a while before I suddenly felt overwhelmed with tiredness. I fought to stay awake, but it was impossible not to give in to the fatigue that washed over me.

'I need to go to bed,' I said.

I tried to usher him to the door, but I never made it.

The next thing I knew it was morning, and I was waking up feeling ill. The man was lying beside me in bed. Feeling dizzy and nauseous, I rushed to the toilet and promptly threw up. I knew this was not like a hangover. It was something different, something more serious.

It was only a few months later, reading about a new trend called 'date rape', that I realized that the man had spiked my drink.

Once again I had allowed my need for intimacy to lead me into a situation of sexual abuse.

When would this ever end?

The breakthrough came in a most unexpected way.

Many of my problems in the area of sexuality stemmed from my experience of abuse by my father, other male members of the extended family and early exposure to pornography. To put it bluntly, as a result of being sexually abused I had come to believe that I had to have sex in order to be valued and loved by men. This was a consequence of a deep father-wound. But I came to see that my father was wounded too and, like me, was on a spiritual journey of healing. This new perspective followed from a change in my own.

After my disastrous night with 'Mr Date Rape', I decided that wrong relationships were not the way to offset my sense of isolation. I began to seek more of God, praying constantly in tongues, reading the Bible regularly, and listening to Christian music. I would go out and pray while I walked. I saw myself in a vision carrying a huge sword as I strode across the moors overlooking our town. I would fight in prayer for the people in my community.

If I ever felt like I fell, I never allowed failure to consume me. I picked myself up, refusing to allow my weaknesses to define me.

God showed me a vision in which I was wearing white, the symbol of his holiness. It gave me so much encouragement to know that because I was forgiven, there was no charge against me and that he saw me as pardoned and pure.

He also showed me a vision in which I was standing in front of large crowds, speaking to them about his love.

As I pressed into more of God's presence, I began to pray more. It was an effort, yes. But it seemed to be working. Even the people who dealt with me at the Job Centre seemed to be more pleasant when I had prayed for them – so I started praying for strangers, acquaintances, and friends.

Most of all, I started praying for members of my family. I knew that my brother and his wife had accepted Jesus as their Lord and Saviour, but I was concerned that the rest of my family didn't know him.

This got me praying for my father.

Then something happened that changed everything. It's a day that I'll cherish for the rest of my life.

I came home one day and realized pretty quickly that I'd locked myself out. Since I lived on the top floor of a two-storey building, I couldn't think how I was going to get into my flat.

Suddenly I remembered that I had seen a long ladder at my brother's house. The problem was my brother was at work and his wife was not strong enough to carry the ladder to her car, tie it down, and bring it over.

Then I had a brainwave. Dad lived in their house. Maybe he could help.

'Da,' I said, when he picked up the phone, 'I'm in trouble. I've locked myself out. Could you bring the ladder over so I can get into my flat?'

'You just caught me,' he replied. 'I was about to go out. I'll fetch the ladder and bring it over right away.'

Not long after Dad arrived with the ladder, and I managed to get into the flat through my bedroom window. I had left it open a crack to air the room. Once I was inside, I let Dad in through the front door. We then sat at the kitchen table and I made him coffee.

We chatted for a while and he told me about some of the problems he had been going through, and the sad story of how he had lost his girlfriend, whom he regarded as the love of his life.

I had heard this story before, but this time there was something different. I could feel the presence of the Holy Spirit as Dad was speaking. That sense of God's presence became heavier and heavier upon me. The kitchen began to look as if it was full of mist.

'Da, do you want to be free from the pains and hurts of your past?' I asked.

His eyes begin to fill with tears.

'Yes, I would,' he replied.

I then gently led him through a prayer in which he asked Jesus to forgive him for his sins, and accepted Jesus as Saviour and Son of God. He then asked Jesus to come into his life. I couldn't believe it. I was so excited. We had come so far in our relationship, but this was the icing on the cake. I had been given the enormous privilege of introducing my own dad to Jesus.

He was born again!

He was a new Christian!

He was on his way to heaven.

From that moment on, the transformation in my dad and in our relationship was profound.

While I had been in America, I had decided to take the initiative and build a bridge between Dad and me. I could have allowed myself to stay in the victim state, but something inside wouldn't let me do that. So I had begun to sow seeds of reconciliation by writing letters to him and phoning him. Then I eventually visited him.

I'm not saying that this was easy. It was an uphill struggle at times. There have been bumpy moments since. But the good of what has happened has far outweighed the bad, and today I know not only that I have forgiven my dad, but that God has too. Today I have a Christian father.

As you will have gathered, my destructive relationship with my father had had a huge influence on all my life. As I have said, I had seen a vision of Jesus sitting at a well, even before I became a Christian, while leading a New Age meditation. This reminded me later of the story in John chapter 4 about Jesus meeting a Samaritan woman at a well in Samaria – a meeting that led to her salvation. When I became a Christian, it was this story that I read through my tear-stained eyes. It was this encounter in John chapter 4 that showed me who Jesus was, and indeed who I was.

I was that Samaritan woman – the woman who was looking for love in all the wrong places.

I was the one who needed to stop looking to men for what I could only find in my heavenly Father.

Becoming a Christian set me on a journey of freedom. I didn't become free straight away. But over time I gradually began to look to my Father in heaven for what I had formerly looked for in men – the love that I'd been searching for all my life.

Along the way, my dad's conversion and transformation was a critical tipping point. When I forgave my earthly father, it brought me into a fresh revelation of my heavenly Father's love.

When I saw my dad come to know Jesus in front of my own eyes, it made forgiveness so much easier. If God could forgive him, then I could too. So forgiveness turned out to be the golden key.

And it also turned out that he wasn't the only one in need of freedom. I was too. We were both locked out of the place where we were supposed to be. But thanks to a ladder, both of us climbed into a whole new level of life and liberty.

That was a miraculous day.

It was a day that only God could have conceived!

30

A 'Whale' of a Time

One of the best known stories in the Bible concerns an Old Testament prophet called Jonah. He was called by God to go to a city called Nineveh to tell the people to repent of their sins or they'd be visited by God's judgement.

Jonah was very reluctant to go. He didn't like the idea of heading for what we would call Iraq (to a city now known as Mosul), and in any case he thought that God was being too kind. There should be no 'turn' for the people of Nineveh, just 'burn'.

Jonah's response to this high and hard call was to head in the opposite direction. He boarded a ship towards a Mediterranean port – the kind of place that today would be the starting point for a cruise. Jonah wasn't in the mood for preaching to people who he thought didn't deserve a second chance.

However, a storm struck his ship. Jonah was down in the bowels of the brig trying to hide at the time. But realizing that the life-threatening gale was a sign that God was none too pleased with him, he jumped ship – literally.

Overboard he went and straight into the mouth of a great fish – many people refer to it as a whale – which just happened to be following them, lurking beneath the waves, its great oesophagus at the ready.

Jonah went down into the belly of this creature and then down into the depths of the ocean.

In fact, his path had been consistently down since he decided that his plan was better than God's plan:

- down into the bowels of the ship
- down into the belly of the great fish
- down to the bottom of the ocean

If there was an example of how disobedience leads to downward mobility, it was Jonah.

Fortunately, Jonah came to his senses. He told God he was sorry for his bad attitude, and – to cut a long story short – God forgave him and redirected him to Iraq.

There Jonah learnt a big lesson: God has compassion on people that we write off.

His mercy triumphs over his justice.

He's kind when we're often not.

Why have I started this chapter with a mini-sermon? It's because the end of my story thus far has a lot of similarities with Jonah's. In fact, you could call me *Joanah* Armin, the woman who ran from God's call.

How did it happen?

You'd think after all the encounters I'd had with God up until now – not least the sense of him watching over me, protecting me, and guiding my path – I would dance cheerfully into my calling.

Not a bit of it! After my dad came to Christ, I started well enough. I was baptized in a friend's pool and that was a glorious moment. I felt special, loved and clean. In fact, it was as if my old life had been washed away, opening up the vistas of God's new future for me.

But instead of walking in obedience to God's call, trusting him and taking whatever risks were necessary, I allowed disappointment and delay to overcome me.

In the end, like Jonah, I ran away from his call and ended up on a ship.

It happened like this.

As a result of a remarkable set of supernatural revelations, I was offered a job assisting a woman who produced Christian TV shows.

This is it! I thought.

Not so, I'm afraid. When it came to the moment of truth, the woman told me that she could only pay me a pittance and that I would have to continue to claim benefits.

'It will be cash under the table,' she said. 'You can keep claiming, but keep quiet about the money I give you. It's our way of getting back at the system.'

I was stunned.

I couldn't believe what I was hearing.

She used Scriptures to try to back up what she was saying – which was not just immoral, it was illegal – and ended up by telling me, 'We need to play them at their own game in order to win.'

Needless to say, I declined the offer of work, even though it was exactly the kind of thing that linked with what I felt passionate about – Christian media.

I cried all the way home – a four-and-a-half hour drive. By the time I arrived, my eyes were nearly swollen shut. I began to feel down – desperately down. I even contemplated ending it all, I was so disappointed. I felt as if I'd had my hopes built up only to have them dashed in the course of one conversation.

In an attempt to pull myself out of my nosedive, I listened to Christian music, read the Bible, watched and listened to DVDs and CDs of great preachers, asked trusted and non-judgemental friends to pray for me, and even went on a Christian retreat. But even though these things helped a great deal, it still wasn't enough to stop my free fall. There was only one thing for it. I would apply for a job working as a massage therapist on a cruise ship. It would be decently paid. It would allow me to travel. It would get me back into sunny climates.

Like Jonah, it was time to run.

I applied for a job and was accepted immediately on board a six-star cruise ship. The company flew me to Venice where I boarded ship. But the ship pretty quickly felt like Sodom and Gomorrah at sea. Most of the crew were having sex. It was next to impossible resisting temptation.

At one point, I began to feel attracted to one of the officers and decided to approach him.

'I'm a Christian,' he said, after a while.

I was gobsmacked.

'But I'm not like you. I don't tell anyone else. I'd be embarrassed to, given my behaviour on board.'

I walked away in a daze.

That was not how I had expected the conversation to go.

But it did something to me. Every time an opportunity for sex presented itself after that, I remembered what the man had said. I didn't want to be someone who was a Christian but too ashamed because of their behaviour to admit it. And I wish I could say I stuck to that resolve, but sadly I ended up giving in and had a string of affairs, each time hating myself all the more, promising never to do it again, until the next time. Eventually I threw myself into my work and gave myself to serving my clients – with whom I had some amazing conversations about God.

But then without any warning the managers on board decided that the tour was too long for some of us, and so we were told to disembark at LA. Instead of continuing on to Hawaii, Tahiti, New Zealand, Australia and Asia, I was put on a plane and flown unceremoniously back to the UK! It was dreadful. I had been spat out, like Jonah, on dry land.

Back in the UK I managed to find a converted beach chalet to rent near my family, and there I started to seek God's perfect will for my life.

It was during this time of pressing into God that I began to sense more clearly than I ever had before that it was time to go and get some training at a Bible college. I had had this feeling before but had fought it vigorously.

Why do I have to go away to study when you can use me here and now, God?

And in any case, I'm not an academic, so why do I have to study at all?

These and other thoughts swirled around my mind, but as I persevered in prayer I began to feel more and more stirred that this was the right way forward. So I found the college prospectuses and started to read, ponder and pray.

I tried to ignore the call for a while by working in an estate agent's to pay my rent. Perhaps the greatest distraction came in the form of a reignited romance which turned, before long, into an engagement. People said my fiancé was going to become a preacher.

It had to be right in that case, didn't it?

But it wasn't. One day while walking on the beach by my chalet, I felt a strong urge to pray for him so we stopped and I heard the Lord say, 'Your faith is like Shadrach, Meshach and Abednego; you're about to go through the fire, but I am with you.' God was referring to the three Hebrew boys we read about in the book of Daniel in the Old Testament; they were thrown into a fiery furnace but God rescued them. It wasn't till a week later I discovered the prayer had been aimed at me and not my then fiancé. Suffice it to say that he was not what he seemed, so the engagement was broken off.

And then I was fired at work.

In fact, in the course of one week I lost my fiancé, my job, my home and my car.

I really was *Joanah* Armin – learning the hard way that running away from the call of God on your life is much more costly than following it ever is.

With everything imploding around me I decided to go for some prayer counselling. I went to a person recommended to me by a friend, and during the session I had a vision of Jesus standing in front of a building and beckoning to me. When I shared it, the counsellor said he'd received a similar vision. The Lord was clearly calling out to me.

And he was calling me to Bible College. It didn't matter to him that I had left school with just a few qualifications. It didn't matter to him that I was scared of study and threatened by academia. He wanted me equipped and prepared for my life's ministry because, as he had said to me before I left America, he had a work for me to do.

After more stubborn resistance – including a brief escape to America – I surrendered to God and put in an application for the London School of Theology in Northwood. I had visited three colleges, but it was this one that I had seen Jesus inviting me to come to in my vision. I applied for grants and then heard from the college. They had accepted me. They felt that the best course for me was the theology degree because they had discerned that my calling was to be an evangelist. All was set fair for me to start my training for God's future plans.

And so I started at the college (LST, as it is known), full of anxiety about my capabilities and fears about making ends meet.

It wasn't always easy. Following God's perfect will is not like sunbathing on a cruise ship. It's more like working on a battleship. My family thought I was crazy. I thought I wasn't clever enough. But God believed in me and I believed in him, and so the bills were paid, the essays were written, and the courses were completed.

God had been behind me. My church had been behind me. My friends had been behind me.

I persevered and I won the prize – a degree in theology at LST!

The whole process had stretched me but I had learnt so much about God, about the Bible and about myself.

I had done some preaching.

I'd received some very accurate words for people in the most random situations.

I had stepped out in faith in all sorts of ways.

At the weekends I had worked in a shop in a local town which was dedicated to bringing the presence of God onto the high street and into the world of retail. It had a spa and so I was taken on as part of a team of massage therapists trained to minister the love of God to stressed people.

I won't lie. There were times when I was tempted to give up college and return to the relative security of massage therapy, but God had told me he was doing a new thing. He was moulding me for something different. So I resisted the pull back to my former occupation, and kept going with my training.

And God honoured my commitment.

To cite just one example, I desperately needed a car at LST, not least for helping to get our preaching team to our engagements. So I started praying.

Out of the blue, a lady whom I had met at a Christian conference – when we were working together on the same ministry team – phoned me to say that she and her husband wanted to bless me with a car! I shouldn't have been surprised. God truly rewards us when we live by faith and in obedience to his perfect plan. When we get back on course, as Jonah did, we find that he's always there for us.

So that's my story so far.

Right now I'm still seeking God for the exact shape of the God-ordained purpose for my life, but I know this: that I was meant to tell my story and that this in itself is part of his plan.

A lot has happened and I remain so humbled and grateful to the Lord for keeping his hand on me. I've stumbled and fallen but I've always got back up, and I know in my heart he has great plans for those who keep putting their trust in him.

Without hope we falter, without love we fall, without faith we fail.

But once we are at home in the arms of the unknown God – who turns out to be the most loving Heavenly Father – he lifts us up, brushes us down, and sets us on our path again.

Epilogue

Two thousand years ago, a Jewish man was walking the dusty streets of the then small city of Athens. As a person who had been brought up to avoid anything non-kosher or unclean, this was radical. Every voice from his past would have been screaming, 'Unclean!' This city was after all a city inhabited by *ha goyim* – the pagans. It was full of ornately carved temples to the Greek gods, graven images and statues depicting Gentile (non-Jewish) deities, the worship of idols and, of course, sexual immorality. This was not a place for a good Jewish boy who had been brought up to be a rabbi called Sha'ul. It was a sin-sodden metropolis – a city where every one of the Ten Commandments was being shamelessly broken. It was the last place a Jewish man would want to set his feet.

But this man Sha'ul wasn't like other Jewish men. He was walking in a different revelation from his peers. He had travelled on a spiritual journey which had brought him to the very epicentre of the Universal Light. So dramatic was the transformation wrought upon him by that encounter that his name had been changed and his mission recalibrated. His new name was now Paul, a Gentile name reflecting his new destiny – to carry the torch of the divine light into the darkest heartlands of the Gentile world. From now on he would be known as the one sent by the God of the universe to open the eyes of those who were spiritually blind and to carry the brilliant torch of truth to *ha goyim*.

Given his new destiny as the apostle to the pagans, Athens was precisely the kind of place Paul felt called to be.

As he strode round the city, Paul looked with a penetrating spiritual discernment at everything around him. He was greatly distressed by the idolatry, of course, but this did not put him off his stride.

After all, Paul was a man on a new mission.

Only a few years before, he had made it his aim to be the staunchest defender of the Jewish faith. In the process, he had sought to stamp out the perversion of the faith which had arisen in some of the synagogues. Jewish men and women had started claiming that a man called *Yeshua* from the town of Nazareth was *ha mashiach* – the long-awaited Messiah (or Saviour). They had become known as the People of the Way. Paul, then addressed as Rabbi Sha'aul, had made it his life's purpose to ensure that this spiritual aberration was stopped in its tracks. For Paul, this Way was no way at all. He was prepared not only to interrogate those who travelled on it, he was ready to have them stoned to death if necessary.

But then his whole universe had shifted on its axis.

Walking the road to Damascus, it turns out he was the one who was stopped in his tracks.

This Jesus, who had been crucified and killed, had been raised from the dead. From heaven, Jesus directed such a searing light into his soul that Paul had been temporarily unable to see.

Only when he realized that he had been spiritually blind was he given his sight back.

Only when he came to confess that this *Yeshua* was the Light of the world was he able to see again.

Then he received a new mandate, to take the Light into the Gentile world, proclaiming the Good News about Jesus.

Since that momentous day, Paul had travelled to cities such as Philippi and Thessalonica, spreading the Light. And then he went to Athens, a hotbed of pagan idolatry. There he spent time finding out about the city's favourite writers, reading works by some of Athens's greatest authors, including Aratus and Epimenides. He also looked at the city's temples, effigies and altars, plumbing the depths of the spiritual quests embedded in their most cherished stories. As he was doing this, he came upon an altar.

To the casual eye, this would have looked like any other religious artefact in the city.

But Paul's eyes were not casual.

They were enlightened.

And as they fell upon this unassuming object, the lights came on in his soul, for the inscription on the stone read *Agnostos Theos* – 'to the Unknown God'. Let's imagine what happened next.

'What's this?' Paul enquired of a street vendor.

'It's one of our most sacred places.'

'Who is the unknown God? Is it Zeus? There are statues and temples to him everywhere.'

'It's not Zeus,' the man replied. 'We Athenians do not know his name.'

'What's the story behind this, then?' Paul asked, pressing a coin in the man's grubby palm.

The man smiled. 'Well, it's like this. Six centuries ago, there was a dreadful outbreak of the plague. It swept across much of Greece and devastated our city.'

'What did the people do?' Paul asked.

'The city authorities thought the plague was a curse from one of the gods. They didn't know which one. They simply assumed the people had offended one of them. So they made sacrifices to all the gods, but none of these offerings did a blind bit of good. The plague wouldn't lift.'

'Ah, I see,' Paul said, rubbing his black bearded chin. 'I suppose they ended up figuring that they'd upset a god that they didn't know.'

'Precisely,' the vendor answered, 'and it was then that Epimenides stepped in with a rather unusual plan.'

'Epimenides, you say?'

'Yes, he was one of our city's most famous philosophers and poets.'

'Indeed,' Paul replied. 'I have been particularly struck by one of his best loved sayings, that "In God we live and move and have our being."'

'That's him,' the vendor said, before adding, 'it was him who told all the local shepherds to release their sheep into the countryside. If any of the sheep lay down, then they were to tell Epimenides straight away. Since it's unnatural for sheep to behave like that, they would know there was something sacred about that plot of land and build an altar there to this unknown God.'

'Let me guess,' Paul interrupted with a knowing smile. 'Some sheep lay down right here, where we are now standing.'

'Dead right,' the man replied. 'Some did indeed lie down here. An altar was constructed straight away. The same sheep were sacrificed and the plague quickly lifted. Ever since then people have venerated the unknown God responsible for the deliverance of our city.'

With that, Paul thanked the man and strode off, heading for the Great Rock of Ares, a small hill just north-west of the Acropolis. Ares was the Greek version of the name Mars, the Roman god of war. There, on what the Romans called 'Mars Hill', the city's elders would hold their council meetings and discuss the latest philosophical and religious ideas.

It was here that Paul was given an opportunity to stand and tell his listeners that the unknown God whom they had been worshipping all these hundreds of years was none other than Jesus.

He is the Light towards which they had been groping.

He is the Deliverer and Healer, the Saviour of the world.

And the truth is he has never stopped being that.

Jesus Christ is the unknown God of the universe.

Now, let me issue you an invitation, just as Paul did on Mars Hill.

You may be on a journey of exploration, a spiritual quest for light and truth.

Let me enlighten you.

Jesus of Nazareth is the Light of the world.

He is the Way.

You may be visiting psychics and astrologers, studying runes and crystals, but it's only in Jesus that you will find what you're truly searching for.

The unknown God of the universe is watching over you as he was over me.

He wants to make himself known to you.

He is longing for an intimate relationship with you.

I travelled a long journey – both physically and spiritually – before I understood this.

There was an altar to the unknown God on the sacred soil of my heart.

Then one day I just knew who it was that I had been longing to meet and desperate to worship.

It was Jesus.

When that happened, I came out of the kingdom of darkness and entered the kingdom of divine light.

You can do this too.

The invitation is for everyone.

The God of the universe is calling you.

How will you respond to his overtures of love?

Prayer

If you would like to become a Christian, then here's a prayer you can say:

Dear Lord Jesus, I believe that you are the unknown God of the universe. I also believe that you have made yourself known to me through Deborah's story. Now I want to get to know you, just as she has. I am deeply sorry that I've looked for you in the wrong places. I repent of my sins and renounce every trace of spiritual darkness in my life. Cleanse me and set me free through the power of your death on the cross. You are the Light of the world, please deliver me from spiritual darkness and come into my life as my Lord and Saviour. I worship you because you rose from the dead and you're alive for ever. I trust you to watch over my life and provide for all my needs. Amen.